If we seek to understand a people we have to put ourselves, as far as we can, in that particular historical and cultural background .... One has to recognize that countries and people differ in their approach and their ways, in their approach to life and their ways of living and thinking. In order to understand them we have to understand their way of life and approach. If we wish to convince them, we have to use their language as far as we can, not language in the narrow sense of the word, but the language of the mind.

Jawaharlal Nehru

THE AMERICAN EXPERIENCE

A Foreign Student Guide

Second Edition

Edited By

Karen M. Holgerson

Pasadena City College

Star

PUBLISHING COMPANY

Belmont, CA 94002

Book design by William R. Dillingham with
additional drawings by Kent Christiansen.

ISBN 0-89863-122-X

PUBLISHING COMPANY
P.O. Box 68
BELMONT, CALIFORNIA 94002
(415) 591-3505

TABLE
OF CONTENTS

FOREWORD

What traveler has not encountered problems in a foreign land? What emigrant has not yearned at least occasionally for his homeland? This book will no doubt touch a responsive chord in the hearts of all wanderers who have had moments of nostalgia even while appreciating and enjoying a new culture.

What foreign student has not thought longingly of his native country even while growing to like the United States? If you are a foreign student, you are likely to find the country and its people, for the most part, friendly and helpful. But what do you do when you have a problem that appears to defy solution? No matter how hard you and your new American friends try, the problem might simply seem to be larger than all of you. Where do you turn? Perhaps this book will help. It was written by people just like you and edited by a professor of English as a Second Language and Intercultural Communication.

The American Experience: A Foreign Student Guide, like many creative ventures, began with just the germ of an idea, a classroom project, a way to encourage foreign students attending school in the United States to learn more about their new American culture. The instructor asked them to write about their experiences after arriving here.

The project put into practice an old principle. What do we write best about? That which we have experienced. How do we get the information so that we can write? Go out and do it . . . see it . . . feel it . . . hear it . . . live it. The students were asked to do exactly that. They were also asked to be painfully frank and write about both their good and bad experiences.

Not only did the students tell about the problems they encountered immediately following their arrival in this country, they began sharing possible solutions to these problems as well. Certainly not all problems show up in the early stages. Some problems erupt long after one gets settled in, at the very moment the student is convinced that he or she has conquered the new environment.

Read the table of contents. Then read about what others experienced while trying to find adequate housing within their budgets, buying a car, ordering a telephone, learning about American etiquette, American holidays, American football, dating, and many other aspects of the American way of life. The stories are revealing.

You may be in the midst of a problem at this very moment that this book might help you with. Or, perhaps you just want to compare your experiences with those of others like you. In any case, I am confident that *The American Experience: A Foreign Student Guide* will be a useful addition to your reference materials.

So that is what this book is all about—foreign students sharing their experiences in adapting to the American way of life. They tell it as it is, as they have seen it—at times unflattering, but open, honest, frank—revealing the American culture as they have experienced it.

This book has many uses—for orientation of foreign students, as a reader for foreign students, for topics foreign students could write about in comparison with or in contrast to their own experience. Even persons who have lived here for some time can profit from this book. A typical reaction to one or another article is something like, "Oh, now that really makes sense!" or "I didn't know that!" These articles can also help students of intercultural communication see the American culture through the eyes of a foreign student: it gives them a rare perspective.

It was a joyful learning experience sharing an office with the editor and watching this project mature. I know that readers will find it a worthwhile learning experience, too, one that will bring its own reward.

Marion S. Murphy
Professor of English
Pasadena City College

PREFACE

Have you ever left your country for a period of time and, upon returning, discovered to your surprise that home wasn't exactly as you had remembered it? If anyone had warned you that such a thing might happen, you probably would have protested. Once familiar people, places, and things might have seemed somehow less familiar, normal events and occurrences less normal. There might even have been moments when communicating was awkward. For a short while, you may have found yourself to be a foreigner in your own homeland.

What you experienced is only a pale reflection of what foreigners experience. Their feelings of strangeness and awkwardness are far more constant, more acute, and more difficult to cope with. They often face major language problems and cultural differences that challenge the values, attitudes, and assumptions that went unquestioned in their own countries. If only all of us, both natives and foreigners, could put on each other's cultural glasses. Our views of each other would become less remote and more empathetic, our interactions warmer and more effective.

Since there is no better place to begin such a process than in one's own national backyard, *The American Experience* begins here in the United States. It explores the realities of American life, as well as the perceptions that non-Americans have of it. Although there have been other guides, how-to manuals, and interpretive works on the American way of life written by individuals, both American and non-American, the approach taken in this volume is unique. It is unique precisely because it does not represent a single cultural point of view. Rather, it is a collection of essays written by non-Americans from around the world who have had a great deal of first-hand experience in adapting to life in the United States. Its editor, a professor of English as a Second Language and Intercultural Communication, is an enthusiastic world traveler who has lived abroad on various occasions.

Since the writers were encouraged to express their own special points of view, no substantial changes were made in the content of the essays. Such changes would have detracted from the charm and the unique insights, as well as from the entertainment and educational value of the total collection. Therefore, the editor and the publisher disclaim any responsibility for the content of the articles.

This particular format has a number of special advantages. It is often surprisingly difficult, if not impossible, for an American to explain American culture to a non-American. Most people are blind to what makes their culture unique and, consequently, find it difficult to pinpoint what foreigners would find difficult to understand or adapt to. When American culture, for example, is seen through the eyes of a non-American, many of those blind spots are revealed.

This is exactly what occurs in this volume. By reading these essays, Americans can see their culture in a new light and find out how they are viewed by non-Americans. Non-Americans, on the other hand, can more quickly and more easily adapt to American life by following the advice and listening to the experiences and insights of those who have successfully gone before them.

The non-American writers of this volume represent a broad cross-section of cultural, linguistic, and educational perspectives. They include young and old, married and unmarried, career people, students, and housewives. As the writers present their views of the United States and of Americans, they often reveal their own cultural values and attitudes as well. Even though the contributors tend to write of personal experiences in large urban communities, most of the articles can be of value to those living in smaller urban and rural communities as well.

This collection of essays is not intended to be a comprehensive work on American life in any sense of the word. It is not meant to function as a how-to manual, although it includes articles that give good advice on coping with various aspects of American life. Finally, it does not show how different cultural groups, such as Asians, Latin Americans, Africans, and Europeans, interact with or see each other. Perhaps future editions will do more of these things.

What exactly does this volume do? It shows clearly how people from different cultures look at the United States and Americans. What originated as an exercise to help non-Americans improve their English skills and make sense out of their American experience turned out to have more value than originally expected.

How can this book best be used? First, it can help non-Americans of any age, religion, or culture adjust to American life. Who would be better qualified to help them in this process than other non-Americans who have been through the experience and know what it is like? *The American Experience,* therefore, can serve as a primary guide in orientation programs for new foreign students, as a supplementary text in intermediate and advanced English as a Second Language classes, and as a source of information on American life for those who are planning a trip to the United States.

Foreign students will learn what to expect from Americans and from their American experience. They will learn how to cope with a new lifestyle, a different culture, an American point of view. These readings offer non-Americans courage in facing difficulties and disappointments in the United States, so that they can turn seemingly negative experiences into positive ones.

Second, *The American Experience* has much to offer Americans. Many of us have spent our entire lives in the United States and, as a result, take that life for granted. It is often difficult to realize that our way of life is not necessarily the norm after all. Realizing this opens us up to the possibility of viewing the world from different cultural perspectives.

The readings offer Americans a rare opportunity to hear both positive and negative criticism about the country they love best. They will begin to appreciate, without becoming defensive, that foreigners may see something in this country that is confusing or unpleasant or that simply doesn't make sense to them. By understanding more about the process that non-Americans go through in adapting to life in the United States, Americans will become more empathetic toward foreigners and, as a result, be more effective in their dealings with them. *The American Experience* not only offers Americans the opportunity to view ourselves and our culture as others from foreign countries do, it also gives us ideas about how we might approach our own experiences abroad as we travel to and live in countries that differ greatly from our own.

Third, *The American Experience* provides topics that will stimulate discussions and conversations, not only in English as a Second Language classes, but in introductory courses of Intercultural Communication, Sociology, and Anthopology as well. Both Americans and non-Americans alike will enjoy discussing many of the issues presented in the essays. Since some issues are somewhat controversial, non-Americans will at times find that they are nodding in agreement, while Americans will find themselves wanting to disagree.

Finally, these essays can be an inspiration to both Americans and non-Americans alike on how best to face experiences in a foreign country with courage and a positive attitude. They suggest ways to enjoy and make the most of the many challenges and opportunities that will come your way. For those unpleasant moments of confusion, conflict, loneliness, and culture shock, they offer good advice: keep smiling, be patient, ask questions, and realize that people of different cultures see the world in different ways.

It is the hope of the editor and the writers of these essays that you, whether you are an American or a non-American, find this volume enlightening, entertaining, educational, and useful.

Karen M. Holgerson

ACKNOWLEDGEMENTS

This selection of readings is dedicated to the many students from other countries who have come, and will continue to come, to live and study in the United States. It is a tremendous challenge, an incomparable opportunity, to obtain a fine academic education in a foreign country, as well as to become educated in a much broader sense. In the process of living in another culture, we have the opportunity of becoming aware of the way the world is viewed through the eyes of another people, while at the same time developing a deeper, more appreciative understanding of our own cultural values and traditions.

Special thanks go, first and foremost, to the foreign students who spent hours upon hours of writing and rewriting to produce these articles in English, their second language. In particular, several students went beyond their own projects to reach out and assist others in the completion of theirs: *Mr. Thomas K. C. Yuan, Ms. Cherry Lim Co, Mrs. Tamira Powell,* and *Mr. Sheng Koo.* Foreign Student Advisor *Wallace Calvert* and his secretary, *Ms. Marilyn Porter,* deserve special acknowledgement for the support, advice, and time spent with students working on projects; in the same way, special acknowledgement goes to *Mrs. Alice Mothershead,* a pioneer in the field of foreign student advising, as well as to two of her community volunteer tutors, *Mrs. Nanci Todd* and *Mr. Robert Greene,* for the patient attention they gave their tutorees as they struggled through their projects.

Warm appreciation is extended to my good friend, colleague, and officemate, *Professor Marion Murphy,* who has been supportive of this project since its inception and has never once lost patience with the many long hours of activity in our office, as well as to the following colleagues who read, gave critical comment and encouragement: Professors *Renee Copeland, Jane Hallinger, Ronald Lanyi, Karen Norris, Lee Reinhartsen, Ben Rude,* and *William Shanks.*

I must also extend my sincere appreciation to *Professor George Hayden* of the University of Southern California for his invaluable editing, as well as for his suggestions in the area of Asian cultures, and to *Mr. G. G. Manross* who offered helpful suggestions through the various stages of publication. In addition, none of this would have been made possible without the typesetting skills and apt suggestions of *Ms. Mary Robillard* nor without the patience of *Ms. Kathryn Perry* through her painstaking efforts in editing and proofreading.

Finally, I would like to thank *Dean Alvar Kauti,* who believed in this project enough to fund its first edition and distribution.

Karen M. Holgerson

CHAPTER 1
GETTING FOCUSED

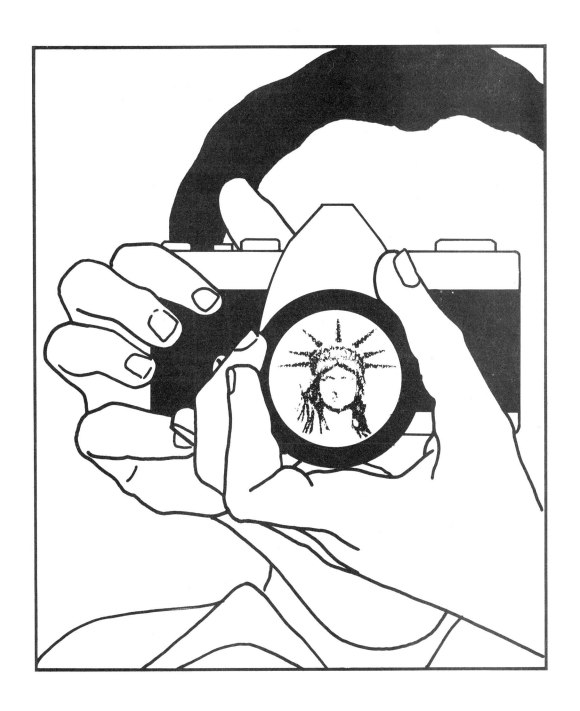

1. INTRODUCTION

The weary, but enthusiastic, foreign visitors finally arrive at their destination after a long journey. Because they will soon be bombarded with strange new sights and smells, images and incidents, that could leave them disoriented and out-of-focus, they will need to get themselves focused in much the same way as they ready their cameras for those first photographs of the new environment. "Seeing" the unfamiliar realities facing them with as much clarity and as little distortion as possible will enable them to interact appropriately and successfully with the new surroundings and its inhabitants.

So it will, no doubt, be for you in the United States. This and subsequent chapters should help you focus in order that you might better face the challenge, experience the adventure, and richly enjoy the unfolding of your American experience. May your experience be a unique and exciting one, and may you rise again and again to meet its many challenges!

THE UNITED STATES: NATION OF IMMIGRANTS

Jennifer Chang
Taiwan

When I first arrived in the United States, I had to wait at the airport for my father's friend to pick me up. He would be an hour late, and I was tired after the long flight from Taiwan, so I looked for a seat to make myself comfortable while I waited for him.

After I had been sitting there awhile, I suddenly became aware of something unusual. People were everywhere . . . all kinds of people . . . in such a variety of colors, shapes, and sizes! Black and white, brown and olive faces were framed by hair-styles of every cut, color, and length. Eyes of every hue, ranging from coal black and liquid brown to bright blue and cool grey, met mine or avoided eye-contact altogether. Some people were amazingly tall; others were short even by Asian standards. Some were noticeably round, others were shapely, still others were straight up and down. This was not at all what I had expected. In my country, people have a much more homogeneous look.

My original belief had been that all Americans looked alike: white skins and brown or blue eyes. These Americans do exist, but they are only part of the picture. I was to discover that Black-Americans and Asian-Americans are just as American as the European-Americans, while none are as American as the original American Indians. Added to their physical heterogeneity is a tremendous variety in their manner of speaking and using English. Different regional and social dialects account for the variety in intonation patterns, vocabulary choices, idiomatic expressions, body movements, and facial expressions.

How could you or I even tell which persons were, in fact, Americans and which ones were not --- that is, which ones were native and which were foreign like you and I are? Which ones spoke a dialect of American English and which ones spoke a foreign-accented English? Making determinations such as these is part of the challenge and fun of getting focused on what life in the United States is all about.

A look at the history of the United States indicates that this country has often been called "a melting pot," where various immigrant and ethnic groups have learned to work together to build a unique nation. Even those "original" Americans, the Indians, probably walked a land bridge from Asia to North America some thousands of years ago. So, who *is* the real American? The answer is that any and all of them are! And *you*, no matter where you come from, could also become an American should you want to. Then you would become another addition to America's wonderfully rich "nation of immigrants."

The United States is currently shifting from being a nation of immigrants of mainly

European descent to one of immigrants from other parts of the world, such as Asia and Latin America. The number of recent immigrants has skyrocketed. Most recently-arrived Asians and Latins come to America, as most other immigrants have come before them, with high hopes for a better future than the one they would have had if they had stayed in their homelands. A number of Asian countries, such as China, Taiwan, Korea, Hong Kong, and the Philippines, have become important new sources of immigrants. With the fall of Saigon in 1975, a substantial number of Vietnamese refugees have added to the diversity of these recent immigrations. Most immigrants from Viet Nam, Cambodia, and Laos are refugees who entered the United States in the 1970's and 1980's. In addition to Asians, Latin Americans (in particular Mexicans and Central Americans) have moved and are still moving in great numbers across the Mexican border. A few stay a while and eventually return to their homes, but most stay permanently and make visits home during holidays and vacations.

What are the reasons for this sizeable immigration? What motives do the new immigrants have? As in the past, strong motivational forces are at work: the desire to escape economic hardship and political oppression in their native countries as well as the desire to seek a better education and a more prosperous life in America, "the land of opportunity." Most immigrants eagerly come to America on a voluntary basis in search of "life, liberty, and the pursuit of happiness."

The desire to start a new life in a new place is noticeable throughout this nation of immigrants. Native-born Americans, as well as new immigrants, believe in the American dream of "equal opportunity for all." The popular "rags-to-riches" stories demonstrate how any one of us can make an American dream come true for ourselves. No matter how poor we are, we still believe that we can achieve wealth and fame through diligence and hard work.

For many Americans who are former immigrants this dream has already become reality. Many of these immigrants have endured hardships in their native lands and continue to do so here. Yet, within a generation or two, they have often managed to raise their social status and economic positions. Although there is sometimes discrimination against foreigners and new immigrants, especially when times are economically difficult, Americans are generally quite accepting and tolerant in allowing new immigrants the same justice and equal opportunity that they have had themselves.

The courage of immigrants to "make it" here has contributed throughout America's history to the vitality and optimism found in this country, which remain two of the outstanding characteristics of most successful Americans. Yet the picture is not always 100% optimistic. Foreigners must struggle to adjust to new ways and different cultural values. Often there is conflict between the ideas they have brought with them from the "old country" and those found in America. Nevertheless, despite the need for such tremendous adjustment, most immigrants learn to adjust to and love their adopted land.

Americans have also learned much from the customs and ideas of the immigrants and are often influenced by them in subtle and interesting ways. Immigrants bring their native cultural, political, and social patterns and attitudes, varied academic and religious backgrounds, as well as their ethnic arts, sports, holidays, festivals, and foods. They have greatly enriched American life. Most especially, the American diet has been delightfully affected by these various immigrant groups. The Italians have introduced Americans to pizza, spaghetti, and antipasto. Americans also enjoy Armenian *shish kebob,* Chinese egg rolls, Japanese *sushi,* Korean *kimchi,* Mexican *tacos*, Swiss cheese, and Thai *satay.* These are just a few of the foreign foods which are apt to appear in the American diet with varying degrees of frequency.

For immigrants from all parts of the world, the United States has been a "melting pot" in which the foreigners have sometimes remained culturally and linguistically what they were in their native lands even as they move toward becoming citizens of the United States, a country whose people share a common cultural outlook and set of values. The melting pot does not melt away all recollections of another way of life in another place — nor should it. On the contrary, immigrants should maintain the languages, skills, religions, customs and arts of their own heritage, even while they are working towards entering the mainstream of American culture.

Some of us have come to the United States not as immigrants but to continue our education or language training, and plan to return to our own countries eventually. Others of us will reside here for the rest of our lives. Whichever category you fall into, the United States offers you a unique opportunity to accomplish your goals and become personally enriched by the varied cultures of many nations around the world found in America. You can visit "foreign" sections in your new city, see foreign films, watch foreign programming on television, and enjoy foreign cultural events. Look for a little Tokyo, a Chinatown, a Koreatown, and Vietnamese, Mexican and Armenian settlements in your city, just to name a few of the many possibilities. Imagine! You can become a world traveler without ever leaving your new city. Continue to enjoy regularly the racial, cultural, and culinary variety to be found in this melting pot called America — even after that first astounding impression at the airport has faded.

IMPRESSIONS OF AMERICA

Cherry Lim Co
Philippines

... open, friendly people ...
... fast-paced life styles ...
... large, open spaces ...
... sprawled-out buildings ...
... expensive supermarkets
with long rows of dog and cat foods ...
... automobiles speeding here and there
on wide, never-ending freeways ...

These are only a few of some typical observations of newly arrived foreigners. Perhaps these observations are some of the first observations you, too, have already made!

During the time you are here, you will continue to modify and refine these and other first impressions. Although such observations can tell you much about your American experience and Americans themselves, they will often tell you more about yourself. You are, whether you acknowledge it or not, a product of your native environment and culture. Therefore, you will "see" a new environment through your own cultural expectations and biases. Being aware of this will help prevent the formation of unfair and distorted judgments about Americans and their culture.

There will be distinct differences between life in your native country and life here in the United States. One major difference will involve the matter of life styles. Personal liberty, freedom, and independence are values which permeate the fabric of American society. Americans are free to select their own jobs, their own religions, their own life styles, no matter how strange, wrong, or illogical they might seem to others. Many of us will observe that Americans have too much freedom, yet many Americans complain they don't have enough!

The right to "life, liberty, and the pursuit of happiness" underlies most American life styles and behavior from the East Coast to the West Coast, in little towns as well as big cities. People will say and do what they want, as long as it is not against the law or physically harmful to anyone. You might see, for example, demonstrations against the President in front of a building where he is making an appearance. On a less obvious scale, you will notice that children leave their parents' homes about the age of 18 with the full consent and encouragement of their parents to strike out on their own. In the same way, grandparents also try to maintain their independence, for they would rather live alone, or in a retirement home, than depend on their families. Grandparents believe their children and grandchildren must live their own lives, just as they have always lived their own.

Another example of the differences is an educational system which is definitely unique to America. It is based on the ideal of equal opportunity for all. Emphasis is on "open access" for all members of society, whether they be rich or poor, young or old, male or female, or handicapped in some way or not. Some people believe that the access is too open and that the quality of education can't be maintained if everyone has to be considered. Elitism exists here, but not to the same degree as in most other countries. It usually does not determine many of the educational programs and institutions here. Another unique aspect is the freedom and consequent responsibility involved in choosing one's own classes and field of study. This is each student's special task. When in doubt about anything, inside class or out, students are expected to ask questions. Students even have the right to disagree over academic policies and grades!

After being here awhile, you will find both advantages and disadvantages to the American way of life. You will have opportunities for a good education, good jobs, personal independence, and freedom. You will also become part of the "melting pot" society whether you want to or not. This will offer you the advantage of knowing many different cultures in addition to the American culture. A disadvantage to this might be some pressure to become more Americanized than you would like to be. Most Americans assume that becoming an American will be your primary goal. Additional disadvantages include culture shock, loneliness, homesickness, and monetary difficulties resulting from America's high cost of living.

At various levels, and in numerous ways, being a foreigner in a strange environment creates in the visitor a feeling of shyness which often deprives him of involvement in activities normally enjoyed by Americans. The new language, customs and traditions will force you, the foreigner, to change some of your attitudes in order to adapt to the American environment. Refusing to adapt will increase the chance of a personality disorder or nervous breakdown. In any case, you will eventually find yourself in a period of some crisis.

In Chinese we have a word, *weiji* (危機), which is the closest translation of the English word *crisis*. Inherent in the meaning of the Chinese word are two other concepts. These are *danger* and *opportunity*. This is exactly the way I have looked upon my American experience ever since first coming here. Although the experience is filled with a certain amount of danger, I have chosen to emphasize the idea of its being an opportunity to learn more about my own culture as well as American culture, to become more mature and self-sufficient, and to face each obstacle and difficulty with a little more courage and flexibility than the time before. In so doing, I have become more able to face adversity and new situations with a positive attitude and appropriate action. Even making mistakes can become a challenge and offer an opportunity for learning and sometimes a little unexpected humor! I have become more adept at making adversity and mistakes good friends of mine.

Although the process of adaptation can be an exciting challenge and opportunity to expand your thinking, eliminate prejudices, and become much more your own person, you must constantly ask yourself these questions. What is truly important to me? Can I change and adapt in this area without selling myself out or compromising my true values? Some of your answers will remain constant; others will change. If you face the challenge of your own unique American experience with patience, perseverance and a positive attitude, you will find, as I have found, that this experience will enhance and enrich all the days of your life.

IMMIGRATION:
HOW YOU COULD BE WELCOMED
TO THE UNITED STATES

Ghadir Khattab
Egypt

Recently, a beautiful young woman of twenty was found dead from suffocation inside an abandoned suitcase of soft fabric following a long international flight to Los Angeles. Who was she? Where had she come from? Why was her body in a suitcase?

The authorities eventually discovered all the answers. She was, in fact, a would-be immigrant who was impatient to await her turn and had decided to enter the country illegally. Her new husband, a legal alien of the United States, had gone home to marry her; he wanted her to be with him, so he had helped make the arrangements for her illegal entry. He was a paid passenger on the same plane as his new wife. Of course, he was horrified and overwhelmed with grief when, at the end of the trip, he went to collect his luggage and found his new wife's lifeless body inside. Several days after her body was discovered by authorities, he himself was dead. He had committed suicide. Some time later his body and hers were returned to their native country for burial.

This true story serves as a tragic example of what can happen to people who attempt to enter the country illegally. Family and friends of the young couple blamed the U.S. Immigration Department for the young woman's death. Although the U.S. Immigration Department has been criticized for a number of mishaps and misfortunes, some of which were its fault, blaming the Immigration Department for this tragedy was a case of not putting the blame where it belonged: with the young couple themselves.

The lesson here is that it is better to enter the U.S. legally, even if it takes more time and effort. If a person wants to come to the United States temporarily or if he wants to become a permanent resident, he has legal ways to do so. Sometimes a person might come to the United States on a temporary basis and decide later on that he wants to stay. Even though he might encounter difficulties along the way, there are ways to accomplish this.

Among the simplest ways to come to the United States is on a visitor's visa or a student's visa. These visas entitle you to stay for only a certain period of time. In the case of a student's visa, you are usually expected to leave once you have completed your education. You must also maintain a minimum of 12 semester units of study to remain eligible under this visa.

What if you have a visitor's visa or a student's visa but have decided to change your status to that of an immigrant? Legally you have many options. The following six options are the most common ones.

1) You might look for somebody to sponsor you. This means that you would be offered a job which could not be filled by an American citizen or resident. The sponsor must advertise the position in the area where the job is being offered. If no one qualifies, you may fill out the appropriate forms required by the immigration office.

2) If you have chosen a field of study in which there is a great need, such as computer science or medicine, you may petition for immigrant status under the Sixth Immigration Code. (Remember that these areas of need change year by year.)

3) You might also consider a visa which allows you to start a business. You can do this by investing a certain amount of money in a business here.

4) You could also consider marrying an American citizen; this would automatically entitle you to become a permanent resident here. However, this would involve a number of cultural and ethical issues which need your careful consideration. Are you in love with the American? Have you considered all of the intercultural difficulties that might arise? Have you discussed and agreed upon the role that families play in your relationship? Have you discussed how money will be used and who will do certain chores? What about the part that religion will play? These answers deserve a great deal of thought and honest communication for you and the American.

5) If a member of your family is a citizen or resident of the United States, you might also more easily and quickly become a permanent resident by applying under that option. The best possibilities with this option occur if your family member is your spouse, your parent, or your child.

6) If you come from a Communist or a Communist-dominated country or are a victim of political persecution, you might also qualify for refugee status.

When in doubt about these and other options, a good immigration lawyer can be most helpful . . . and costly. Most immigration lawyers will charge you between $75 and $200 per hour for the work they do. Yet a good lawyer can make the way a lot easier for you. If you are one of those who cannot afford a lawyer, try to consult somebody at your university or college where the personnel experienced in such matters might be able to help you.

In spite of the rather precise rules and regulations, problems often come up when dealing with the United States Immigration and Naturalization Service. The most common problem is the language barrier. A lot of immigrants find it difficult to communicate with immigration personnel, who usually only speak English. Often the forms are in English, too, unless you visit a consulate in your own country. Always read carefully and understand every word before you sign anything, whether it be in large or small print. *Always ask* if there is something you don't understand. If you don't know English well enough, take somebody along to translate.

Another common problem is the long wait for your visa turn when you are from a country which has a large number of immigrant applicants. Each country has its quota of visas, so be patient and persevere.

Additional problems which you may encounter are the ones caused by the Immigration Service itself. The most common difficulties are the loss of applicants' papers, delays in processing the papers, and unintended mistakes, large and small. I, myself, experienced the first problem: the loss of my papers. My application and papers were discovered missing after I had waited patiently for seven months. When I became persistent, Immigration officials answered me in this way: "Your papers cannot be located." There was no apology or explanation. I felt devastated. The simple truth that I had to face was that my papers were lost. This was for me just a matter of bad luck.

I learned from that experience to always keep important documents and copies of applications and letters in a safe place. I also learned to keep a complete record of dates and names of people talked to and to send all official papers by registered mail in order to have proof of receipt. If you do this until your alien registration card is in your hand, you will ensure fewer difficulties.

As far as delays are concerned, a student in my college told me that she had waited eight years for her alien registration card. She told me she hadn't paid attention to some seemingly insignificant details, and an unnecessarily long delay resulted. Always pay attention to those small details. Your papers, like hers, may be delayed for something as insignificant as an unclear fingerprint.

Some applicants for immigration make a lot of mistakes; so do the Immigration employees themselves. Some ask for unrequired papers, others write down wrong information, and still others issue people incorrect visas. Be careful and clear in filling out your application form. Write your name with every letter exactly as it is on your legal documents, such as passport and birth certificate. Be aware of your rights and be prepared to fight for them. Use your intelligence to your advantage, for there is always a way out of any difficulty.

Immigrating to the United States is not always an easy or simple process. If you decide that it is worth the effort, learn from my experiences and from those of others who have done it successfully. Know your options, be meticulous in filling out forms and in keeping duplicate records, and seek the appropriate help when you can't accomplish it yourself.

CHAPTER 2
SETTLING IN

2. INTRODUCTION

Now that you have survived your first encounters with Americans and American life and accumulated your first impressions of the city where you will be spending time, you might now be one of those who will be staying for a while. If so, this chapter is for you!

"Settling In" concerns taking the necessary steps to find yourself the right place to live and to get the conveniences that will make for a more comfortable life here. This part of your adjustment to life in the United States is a most important task and a substantially difficult one; having some clear ideas about how best to proceed will make the task less difficult and the results more desirable.

Most of the articles in this chapter offer important suggestions along these lines. Consider the writers of these articles to be the voices of experience! They have lived successfully through this part of their American experience. Hopefully, they will help you move through your experience more easily than they did by helping you avoid some of the mistakes they made.

There will probably be vast differences between the way things are done in your homeland and the way things are done here. Now is the time to anticipate and accept the differences as you settle as comfortably and happily as possible into your new American home.

FINDING THE RIGHT PLACE TO LIVE

Chi Leung
People's Republic of China
and
Tji Jong Ong
Indonesia

Many foreign students have come to the United States to gain a good education and experience American life. Even though they usually have the best of intentions, they often fail to get the right information to guide them in making a choice to match their individual needs and resources. As a result, they may encounter problems in the early months of their stay and find their expectations difficult to fulfill. A major problem which they must solve is finding the right place to live.

It is not surprising that many newly arrived foreign students feel totally helpless when they first try to find a place to live in the United States. Some had thought that they would enjoy their stay here, but after they arrived, housing problems caused many headaches and upsets. However, foreign students should not give up even when things seem complicated and difficult. The big choice for foreign students is whether to stay in a dormitory, in an apartment (alone or with roommates), or in an American home.

Dormitories are, no doubt, the most convenient places to live since they are usually located on campus not far from classrooms, libraries, and cultural events. Yet they can be noisy, and this can interfere with studies. In addition, some schools do not even have dormitories. If your college or university does not have dormitories, two choices remain; you will either have to live in an apartment or in an American home.

I remember that when I first arrived in this country, I had quite a difficult time finding the right place to live. My college, like many colleges, did not have dormitory facilities; therefore, I had to either live with an American family or rent my own apartment. I decided to rent.

In the beginning, I moved into a three-bedroom house and shared the rent with three young Americans. At first, everything seemed to work out well, and I was pleased with myself for having found a good and pleasant place to stay, as well as having arranged a means to practice my English. After a short while, I began to feel mentally and emotionally isolated. Even though I had tried my best to adjust, bridging the cultural barriers was time-consuming, frustrating, and not as successful as I had hoped. My situation soon led me to the decision to find another place to live.

After two weeks of confusion, telephone inquiries, and door-bell ringing, I was lucky to find another apartment near the college. I also found new roommates, this time from my own country. With the same ethnic and cultural background, we were able to work out everyday problems, as well as help each other solve academic and personal problems. In addition, living in such an environment helped me overcome the mental and emotional isolation caused by the cultural differences of the previous situation. It contributed to my general happiness and well-being. The fondest memories of my college days in America have been these.

As you can imagine, looking for the right place to live is often a frustrating and time-consuming task. Since it is human nature to get harried and frazzled under pressure, many mistakes are made at this stage which can later turn out to be costly in time, money, and emotion. Therefore, it is wise for us to stay cool, calm, and collected in order to get ourselves organized for the job at hand.

What is the best way to approach the situation? First of all, collect all the rental information you can get from the various sources available. A few good sources are the housing or apartment ads in the classified sections of local newspapers as well as the notices on bulletin boards in and around the foreign advisor's office. Before you start looking, decide what sort of area you want to live in, how much rent you can afford to pay, and how long you plan to stay there.

When you first begin to look for an apartment, don't rush your decision. Since some apartments are located in high crime areas, be careful about the neighborhood you pick. Have you ever noticed that most places that are located in bad areas have bars on the house windows? Houses in good community areas usually don't have such window protection. Another way to get information about the neighborhood is by asking the police officers who patrol the area, as well as people who work or study at your school. They can usually tell you what areas are low-income areas.

In addition to looking for a good area, you may also want to consider getting a place near some busy streets. This is especially necessary if you have to do your own grocery shopping and do not have any means of transportation. You may also want to be near shopping and entertainment centers.

You will probably want to find out what kind of facilities are provided at a given location. Is the apartment furnished? Are a refrigerator, a stove, and other major appliances provided? Is there parking for your car? Some apartments may provide laundry facilities, while others do not. Some may even provide swimming pools, pool tables, spas, gymnastic rooms, and special entertainment events. Unfortunately, these types of places will generally cost you more. As the saying goes, "You get what you pay for."

In addition to the above, budgeting for expenses is highly important. Of course you should try to get the nicest apartment *within* your budget range. Prices are usually based on the location, the facilities, the number of bedrooms, and the age and condition of the building. Since the rent is often set according to the area and facilities of the apartment, the location with convenient access to school or shopping centers may cost you a bit more. The extra cost is worth it to the newcomer who is not familiar with his new environment.

Other than the rent itself, you might have other expenses. The landlord will probably ask you to pay the first and last month's rent before you move in. Some will also require that you pay a security deposit at that time. A security deposit is held against potential damage to the property and is normally refundable if the property is left in good condition. The landlord may also specify that you will have to stay for at least a certain number of months; if you do not meet this requirement, you are bound to be penalized financially. You should always find out how much notice you need to give the landlord before moving out.

Students living in an apartment usually have to pay for their electric, water, gas, and phone bills. However, some landlords may already include the electricity and water in the rent. Finally, the condition of the apartment contributes a great deal to a pleasant stay. Is it in good condition . . . toilet, faucets, plugs, and windows? If you are like me, you would not enjoy the fresh air which broken windows provide; therefore, check the place over to avoid problems caused by defects in the apartment facilities and grounds. And be sure to ask a potential landlord for answers to these important questions before making your decision.

Because it is often quiet and lonely living in an apartment alone, consider having a roommate. This is often a good way to prevent or cure loneliness, and, at the same time, to cut down on expenses. While splitting the rent and utility bills with roommates is advantageous, having to give up the privacy and freedom of living alone can be disadvantageous for some. Another disadvantage might occur if your roommate caused any damage or failed to pay his rent; you could be held responsible by the landlord unless your roommate has entered into a separate rental contract with the landlord before moving in. It is wise to have an agreement written down, clearly defining all the duties and responsibilities that you and your roommate have whether you have signed an agreement with the landlord or not.

Once you decide to rent a particular apartment, you will be faced with either an oral or written agreement. Most agreements are written and, in the United States, are always preferable to oral ones. Some written agreements are called leases. Leases involve the most "red-tape" because they have rental time requirements. Most foreign students would do well to avoid such agreements. All written agreements, including leases, detail the parts of the agreement and eliminate the potential problems likely to occur later. When considering any kind of written agreement, read it carefully and ask any questions to clarify what is not understood. Before you sign it, negotiate any and all points of difference between you and the landlord.

Instead of living in an apartment, students can also choose to live with an American family. Living in an American home can save a student many living expenses, as well as help him improve language skills and build cultural expertise. If you decide to live with an American family, you should also look around first before deciding which family to stay with. Find out whether the family has any pets which you don't like. Do you get a private room and bathroom in the house? Also check to see how the room is furnished. Next, find out whether meals are included, and, if they are, how many and what kind. In addition, you may wish to take into consideration how big the room and the house are. You may also want to find out from the family if you can bring any guests home and during what hours. Can they stay overnight? How close will you be to school? Always *ask* before deciding!

It it sometimes difficult to decide where to live. All of us have different thoughts and feelings about living styles. From my experience, living in an apartment gives more privacy and freedom than living with an American family or in a dormitory. On the other hand, living in an apartment can increase your living expenses if you are living alone. You may also feel lonely in an apartment and not like having always to do your own cooking and cleaning. Finally, living in an apartment will not improve your English skills and broaden your knowledge about American culture.

You should now have some good ideas about various housing alternatives in the United States and how to decide on the best housing for you. Take great care in finding a place to live which you will like and which will meet your needs while you are here. Choosing your housing carefully will contribute to your success and happiness while you are in the United States.

ENCOUNTERING MY NEIGHBORHOOD

Rosa Flores de Avila
Peru

I lived in my country, Peru, all my life until four years ago. When I learned that I had to write an essay about the neighborhood where I live now, my thoughts flew back immediately to Peru, my former neighborhood, my former home. I realized I have yet to cut my umbilical cord.

To write about this matter aroused in me special and contradictory feelings. It is as if a traveling salesman were asked to talk about his home and talked instead about the hotel where he spends one or two nights during his business trips. I feel that way about my new neighborhood here.

I discovered that I could write more easily about all of this at a place in a corner of my apartment that is very familiar to me: my desk, a place where I spend most of my time and where I am surrounded by familiar faces (photographs from home), my tape recorder, books, and dictionaries, a place where I have spent pleasant moments . . . and difficult ones, too, trying to learn a new language.

There is another place where I can write too. That place is the public library in the downtown area of my city. It was the first place that I came to know when I first came to the United States. I went there almost every day, and I felt at ease there. The time passed, and I learned by heart all the Spanish books on the shelves in the foreign language section. There are other places which I consider almost like my own home: the different schools that I have attended and am attending to learn English and get an education.

Right now I am thinking about my apartment again, and several images appear suddenly before my eyes: my plants, my goldfish which swim freely and contentedly within the ambiance of their very own fishbowl, a plate of fresh doughnuts . . . then, too, the lovely old lady who is the manager of the building and a very good friend of mine; she gives me doughnuts or other treats almost every day.

To the right of my apartment live our neighbors, the Russians, who are always trying to convince my husband and me to attend their church. To the left, there is a building so crowded with people that they are almost coming out through the windows . . . along with the sounds of noisy music, obscene words, and strange food odors.

Across the street from me lives a smiling Filipino man who always asks my husband and me to visit his home and have coffee with him. In the garden in front of his house a large sign is posted: *Income Tax.*

On the corner, there is a gay club. Its opening caused quite a bit of commotion in my neighborhood some time ago. The Russians began to visit their church more often as a result. Our manager, the lovely old lady, enjoyed herself by finding it all exciting . . . good for her! She kept bothering the police with her complaints against that "notorious" bar. My husband and I exhausted all the means at hand to avoid hearing the noise from their loud parties. We put cotton in our ears; my husband even wore headphones for a time, but all our attempts were fruitless.

In a house down the street from us lives a group of hippies . . . I guess that would be the best way to refer to them, keeping in mind their distinctive style of dress and my superficial observation of their life styles.

Our neighborhood butcher also emerges in this remembrance parade; he is really a nice fellow. I often exchange a little vocabulary with him: *pechuga* . . . breast, *alas* . . . wings, *una libra* . . . a pound. Another character very important in my life is the mailperson . . . or should I say mailgirl? The female cat often appears, too, filling the neighborhood during special times of the year with her queer cries.

To make real all these faces and situations has been almost a miracle, but I can at last define my neighborhood. My neighborhood is my desk, doughnuts, fish (one black, one red), mailgirl, gays, taxes, fried meat odors, *"pinche escuincle!"* (damned kid), a cat in rut . . . and an old song entitled: "I Will Survive."

LIVING SUCCESSFULLY WITH AN AMERICAN FAMILY

Chan Hou Loi
Macao

Would you like to improve your English and understand American culture better? My friend Kimi has lived with an American family for several years now. She has lost much of her Japanese accent, has become quite at home here, and continues to enjoy her American experience.

Living with an American family can offer foreign students opportunities for a multitude of positive results. Even though most foreign students have studied English in their native countries, most of them have trouble communicating in English and adjusting to American life.

By living with an American family, you will get to know something about the way its members live, think and feel, the roles they play in family life, the social ties and obligations that they honor, and the kinds of situations they find humorous. You will also improve your English in a quick and easy manner. As you broaden your restricted knowledge of slang and increase your everyday vocabulary, you will communicate with more confidence and ease.

Living with an American family usually offers you the opportunity to adjust to American culture and customs and to feel more at home here. You can even learn the way they cook . . . or don't cook! At the same time, you will also be giving Americans an opportunity to learn about you, your country, and your culture.

Living with an American family is also advantageous to you in other ways. You usually save money by paying less rent than you do living in an apartment of your own. If you really want to save money, maybe even earn some, you can live with an American family who wants you to do some work for them; you can perhaps even get free room and board in exchange for that help and might even earn some extra pocket money! In addition, you probably won't have to worry much about food preparation or going to the market; both are time-consuming and problematic. This will afford you more time to spend on your studies.

Yet your experience will not always bring only advantages and enjoyment. What are some potential disadvantages? First of all, at times you might feel left out if your American family wants to spend time alone without your being included. Americans value their privacy and independence, and they may expect you to understand. Secondly, cultural conflicts will no doubt arise, since it is difficult to deal harmoniously with human beings even if they come from your own culture, let alone a different one. In these matters, be patient, try to understand them, and ask questions when you do not understand.

Sometimes you may not feel relaxed and carefree but will feel that there is too much tension or noise, especially if that particular household has young children. But as you know, no roses exist in this world without thorns! Sometimes, you will bother them too. Because occasionally there will be conflicts and failures in communication due to cultural differences, it is important for you to get an American family whose members are willing to be helpful, understanding, and respectful of you, and considerate of points of view different from their own.

In the process of enhancing our well-being while living with an American family, and getting rid of negative aspects, we should try to communicate with the American family members when there are disagreements or problems. Americans usually prefer direct communication. Never assume that they can read your mind; you will probably have to explain tactfully any dissatisfactions you feel.

Always do your part in household chores and activities. Most American families operate this way. Always remember that you are the foreigner, that you are in their home and in their country. Avoid speaking your native language in their presence. It is considered rude, and they will, perhaps, feel left out.

Yet, what happens if you happen to move in with a family who is rude or unpleasant or is taking advantage of you? You will need to look for a new house immediately. If you stay, you might develop a jaundiced impression of Americans and ruin your American experience.

Living with an American family can be beneficial, fun, and enriching. Most American families will appreciate your being involved in their activities and will want you to enjoy a home atmosphere that *includes* you. If so, let them claim you as their "adopted" son or daughter. For you, in turn, can claim them as your American father and mother. Listen to their advice, value their encouragement and support, for you will learn much from them about how best to succeed in American life. This will help you fulfill your goals in the United States — and reward you with an American experience that is lasting, warm, meaningful, and full of good memories.

GETTING YOUR AMERICAN TELEPHONE INSTALLED

Linda Wibisono
Indonesia

A telephone is one of the most important tools for communication in the United States. A telephone saves time, finds information, and brings you help in case of emergency. Some homesick students will also be delighted when they call their families and friends overseas and hear familiar voices in a familiar language. Friends and family members can be brought into your American living room by just dialing a few numbers.

Most everything will seem strange and confusing to newcomers in this country. The installation of a telephone is no exception. It is difficult and costly to get one installed here. Problems which students encounter usually result from the language barrier and procedures which are unfamiliar. Don't let the language get you down; use the language skills you have to ask necessary questions about the procedures.

To get your telephone installed in the easiest way possible, go to the nearest telephone company office in your area or ask someone what the company telephone number is and call it. Someone from Customer Service will explain what kinds of services you can have and the prices of each. Customer Service will tell you how to find out whether you have an existing telephone line in your place or not. If you don't have one, you will have to pay quite a bit of money for a new installation. Most places, however, will already have a line installed.

After Customer Service explains everything, you have to decide what kind of service, as well as what style of telephone, you want. You can rent or buy the telephone set of your choice; again Customer Service should explain your options to you.

There are also some special services to consider in addition to the usual telephone service, which cost extra:

Call Waiting — This service enables you to receive other phone calls even though you are on the line with someone else. You just have to put your first party on hold by pressing the receiver button in order to answer the other party. Then you press the receiver button again, and you will go back to your first party.

Call Forwarding — This service you use when you are away from home and don't want to miss some of your important calls. You can have your calls forwarded to any place you like. To do this, you first have to dial the code number which is given by the phone company; then you dial the number where you want the calls transferred. After you hear the sound (tut . . tut) your calls will be transferred. When you return home, you can cancel it. To do this, you dial a different code number; after you hear the same sound twice as before, you know that your call forwarding has been cancelled.

Three Way Calling — This service allows you and two other friends to talk simultaneously. While you are talking with one party, and you want to call a second party to join in on the conversation, all you need to do is to press the receiver button twice. The first press is to hold the first party while you call the second party. The second press is for the second party to join your conversation. So, if you have a class project involving more than two people, you can all have a conference together on the phone.

How long will it take you to get your telephone installed? It depends on how busy they are; it normally takes two to seven working days until the line is installed.

After your phone is installed, there is one word of warning. Always pay your bill on time! If you don't, you may find your phone disconnected; to reconnect it again you have to go to the local office and pay a deposit. The money will be held for a one-year period. Not only does reconnecting cost you money, it costs you time and inconvenience as well.

Knowing how to get your telephone installed and how to use the different services will make your life in America easier, more enjoyable, and more fulfilling.

USING THE TELEPHONE

(How to Make the Telephone Your Friend)

Silvia Tamira Powell
Brazil

As happens to many foreigners during their first months in the United States, I wasted time and money and got lost and tired, until I decided to make the telephone my friend. After I learned the difference between the American and Brazilian telephone systems, I became a phone addict. Now I can live without a car and be short of money, but I cannot live without a telephone of my own. It helps me to get information, to make appointments, to request catalogs and application forms, to buy merchandise, and to order carry-out food. It helps me in emergencies. It keeps me in contact with my relatives and friends, here and in my country. So, if the telephone can do these things for me, it can do the same and more for you. You can take advantage of the telephone and get it to help you. It can save you time, money, and a lot of trouble. As an added bonus, you can practice your English, too.

Even though the American telephone system is easy, the pay telephone is different from that in many other countries. For local calls, 20 cents have to be inserted, which allows you to speak for an unlimited time. In addition to local calls, you can make long distance calls from a pay phone. You have to insert two dimes and dial *1-area code-number*. The operator or a recording will tell you how much money will be necessary to complete the call. In case of a recorded answer that you cannot understand, dial "O" and the operator will help you. Be prepared to have enough coins. A good idea is to ask the operator the rate before you make your call. If you are going to make an international call, the process will be the same as for a long distance call. The only difference is that you have to dial *011* for a direct call and *01* for *operator help - country code - area code - number*. But if you want to make a person-to-person call, you have to dial the number *0* instead of the number *1* and give the operator your name and the name of the person with whom you want to talk. In all cases, when you use the pay phone, if the amount of money inserted is less than the cost of your call, after you hang up the operator will call you back and ask for the exact amount of money.

It can happen that you are short of money. In this case, you can make a collect call. The process for a collect call is the same as that of a person-to-person call, with only one difference: you don't have to insert a single coin. There are two more alternatives if you are out of coins. One of them is to charge the call to a third number. This means that you can ask the operator to charge the call to your number at home. If you don't have your own telephone, you can make some kind of arrangement with one of your friends or the family where you are living and pay them back later. The other alternative is to use a telephone credit card if you have one. You have to give your telephone credit card number to the operator.

The private telephone is less complicated than the public telephone. The process of all calls is the same but even simpler than that of the coin phone, except, of course, you don't have to insert coins to make your phone call. If you want to send a written message instead of making a call, dial the number *1(800) 325-6000* and the operator will send your message. This telegram will be charged on your telephone bill.

Learning all about the use of the telephone is very important for many reasons. Along with practical and social aspects, the telephone can help you in case of fire, accident, sudden illness, or burglary. Keep on hand the telephone numbers of the Fire and Police Departments, the paramedics, and that of a close friend or relative. Your consulate's number should also be kept on hand, in case of some immigration problem, a stolen or misplaced passport, or any other kind of emergency that needs consular help. These telephone numbers are easily found in the telephone book of your area.

The directory (telephone book) is a great help, but here again, it can be different from that in your country. The white pages list the names in alphabetical order. In case of persons, look for the person's family name, and in case of commercial telephone numbers, look for the first name of the company, bank, or department wanted. The yellow pages, on the other hand, list the commercial numbers by category in alphabetical order. For example, if you are looking for an airline telephone number in the yellow pages, look for the airline's name in the air travel section; or, if you are looking for the address of a health resort or spa, look for the spa's name in the health club or resort section. The yellow pages are very useful because they provide not only telephone numbers but also addresses and other information about the names published there.

Unfortunately, your directory book will only list the telephone numbers in your area. For numbers in your area, you can also call for information by dialing *411*. For numbers out of your area, dial *1-(area code of the city you are calling)-555-1212*. If you don't know the area code of the city, dial "O" for the operator and ask for the area code of the city wanted. The operator will also help you with information for foreign countries.

Whenever you need the help of the operator, dial "O". The most common situations that require an operator's help are difficulties in completing a call, emergency calls answered by recorded messages, a line that seems always busy, calls answered by recordings which are hard to understand, coins not returned when the call does not go through, and calls to countries not yet using direct dialing. The operator is there to help you; don't be embarrassed if your accent is strong, for operators are trained to help people, no matter how they speak or what country they come from. Most operators are very nice people.

If you are concerned about your money, before a long distance call you might ask the operator about special rates or check the phone book. At certain times of the day, usually evenings and holidays, rates are lower. But be sure that you are not going to awaken somebody at 3:00 in the morning only to save money. So, if you are not sure about the time difference between here and the place you are calling, ask the operator.

Now that you just finished reading about how useful a telephone can be, how about getting your own telephone? If you want to have a telephone, first go to a nearby telephone store. The only thing necessary is to have your identification card and an address. You can buy or lease the equipment. Usually, a telephone company employee will install your telephone for a fee. Easy, isn't it?

And, if while reading this article, you were wondering what time it is or what the weather will be like this weekend, you can get that information free of charge by dialing the numbers listed in the yellow pages under the time and weather listings.

I hope that the telephone becomes your friend as it has become mine, and that it helps you for any and all occasions. I also hope that you will never need to use it for an emergency call. Good luck with your new American friend, the telephone!

Notes:
- Use the following names to help you clarify misunderstood words, names, and spellings on the telephone:

A as in Apple	K as in Katherine	U as in Uniform
B as in Boy	L as in Larry	V as in Victor
C as in Cat	M as in Mary	W as in William
D as in Dog	N as in Nancy	X as in X-ray
E as in Edward	O as in Oscar	Y as in Yankee
F as in Frank	P as in Peter	Z as in Zebra
G as in George	Q as in Queen	
H as in Henry	R as in Richard	
I as in Indian	S as in Sam	
J as in Jack	T as in Tom	

- Use the following list of telephone numbers as a ready reference. If you wish, make a photocopy and keep it in a convenient place near your telephone.

"O" .... *for operator*

411 .... *for local telephone number information*

1-area code-555-1212 .... *for non-local telephone number information*

911 .... *for emergency telephone calls (police, fire, paramedics) in most areas of the United States.*

1-area code-number .... *for long distance direct dialed telephone calls within the United States*

011-country code-area code-number .... *for direct dialed long distance telephone calls outside the United States*

01-country code-area code-number .... *for operator assisted long distance telephone calls outside the United States*

1-800-325-6000 .... *for sending written messages (mailgrams, cablegrams, telegrams) through Western Union*

- The price of a local phone call may vary in different areas and with different telephone companies.

ARTICLE
2.6

USING AMERICAN STYLE TABLE MANNERS

Wu Lee-Hwa
Taiwan

In some Asian countries holding a bowl of rice up to the mouth and "shoveling it in" with chopsticks would be considered acceptable; in others, slurping noodles or hot tea might be appropriate. In America, both would be considered crude and ill-mannered. These are only two illustrations of how table manners vary from country to country.

All cultures have their own particular etiquette for eating. As with most cultural conventions, people judge others on how well they follow the rules or conventions. Therefore, having the "correct" table manners wherever you happen to live is important. Most people are able to enjoy their food better when eating with others who follow the same conventions or rules of eating. Making loud noises or dropping food on the table are unacceptable in most cultures, but the utensils that are used, the formalities that are followed, and the foods that are served differ greatly from place to place. Some cultures even consider eating a time for enjoying friendship and pleasant conversation, while others prefer silence in order to concentrate on the enjoyment that eating fine food brings.

Let's take a look at some basic points in American dining procedures. We are not talking about eating out in restaurants, or about big, formal dinner parties, but rather about the accepted rules for proper eating habits that most American families follow when seated at home for a meal.

Some families like to say a prayer of thanks before beginning to eat. This prayer is called grace. A fairly typical form of this prayer is as follows:

"For what we are about to receive, may the Lord make us truly thankful. Amen."

Usually grace is said only on special occasions or for Sunday dinners, but some families say it daily or before each meal.

The table is usually set in a special way. Setting the table properly can be a matter of great pride to the lady of the house, especially when there are guests for dinner.

Setting the Table

This is not only a matter of pride for a hostess but an added pleasure to help guests eat their meals.

A. Placement of silverware

    1. Place the knife to the right of the plate with its cutting edge toward the plate.

2. Place the spoon with its rim up to the right of the knife.
3. Place the fork to the left of the plate.
4. If a butter spreader is used, it should be placed across the top of the bread and butter plate.
B. Placement of glasses, napkins, and chairs
1. The glass belongs at the tip of or just to the right of the knife.
2. The napkin is placed to the left of the fork and one inch from the table edge.
3. Each chair should be placed with its edge just under the table.

Eating Properly

Most American families use the typical American style of eating. To eat in this style, you generally hold the fork in your right hand. If you have to cut a piece of meat, put the knife in your right hand and the fork in your left hand. Hold the meat on the plate with the fork while you cut one or several pieces with the knife. After you finish cutting the meat, put the knife across the upper right portion of your plate. Transfer the fork to your right hand and lift a piece of meat to your mouth. To cut another piece of meat, you repeat the process.

Remember these simple rules:

1. Use your fork for most food.
2. Use your knife only for cutting and spreading.
3. Cut your salad with a knife only if it's necessary.
4. When you've finished, place the knife and fork parallel to one another on the right side of the plate. This means that you've finished this portion of the meal.

Buffet Dining

When you entertain guests, don't feel that you have to have a sit-down dinner like the one mentioned. Americans enjoy the buffet-style dinner, and it's easier on the host or hostess. A buffet style dinner is a good opportunity for guests to circulate and enjoy their meal at the same time. Guests can wander from one group to another as they serve themselves different courses.

The buffet table, although not as formal as a sit-down dinner, can be made to look attractive and inviting. Brightly patterned tablecloths or elegant white ones will set the mood that you are trying to create. Add a bouquet of flowers, candles, or fancy napkins as the mood hits you. Make sure, however, that there is a place for all guests to sit down should they want to.

Eating Special Food

Spaghetti — The best way to eat long spaghetti is with a fork and a large soup spoon. The spoon is held with the left hand while the fork is held in the right one. Pick up a few strands of spaghetti with your fork and place them against the bowl of the spoon. Now wind them slowly into the spoon until the strands are wound around the fork.

Baked Potato — If you are served a baked potato that is uncut, cut it with your knife and then break it open with your fingers. After adding sour cream, butter, or seasoning, use your fork to lift the white part of the potato while you hold the potato firmly with the left hand.

Cake — If you are having cake for dessert, there are several possibilities for ways to eat it. Using your fork is always proper. If it's small and non-messy, you can even eat it with your fingers. Many Americans will do exactly that. If it is large, sticky, filled with cream, or covered with lavish frosting, use your fork; with ice cream, use a fork plus a dessert spoon.

Finger Foods — These foods are dry or firm enough to be eaten with your fingers. They include bread, rolls, crackers, toast, most sandwiches, fried chicken, crisp bacon, corn on the cob, potato chips, cookies, and candies.

Smoking

If there are ashtrays on the table, the hostess probably would not mind if you smoke after the meal is over. But, before lighting a cigarette, pipe, or cigar, ask the other guests for permission. You could ask: "Do you mind if I smoke?" Most people will say, "Go ahead." However, if there are no ashtrays, this is a good indication that smoking would not be welcomed. It would be better not to ask at all, especially since fewer and fewer Americans are smoking these days.

Good Advice for Foreign People

If certain dishes at a dinner party are new to you, just remember to follow the hostess' lead. Always try a little of everything even if it looks uninviting.

Wherever you go in the world, sharing a meal or a drink is a most common way of socializing. It is usually a time to relax and enjoy good conversation and companionship. Therefore, it's important to display good manners and to provide an attractive and pleasant environment. Silence might be considered rude, so help keep the conversation going by asking questions and talking. Following the proper etiquette is like the oil of society . . . it makes life smoother and more enjoyable.

USING YOUR AMERICAN TV WISELY

Tai Ting San
Taiwan

For foreign students and immigrants, American television has both positive and negative aspects. As for the positive aspects, most of us can gain much from watching a certain amount of television. It can help us learn American English, become familiar with American culture and everyday life, keep up with current events, get information about new products, and enjoy inexpensive and convenient entertainment at home. Keeping these advantages in mind when we choose our programming can only benefit us.

As for learning the language, television offers us a lot of listening practice in American English. We can pay more attention to what people say and how they say it. We can listen to a variety of dealects of American English, both social and regional. All of this will serve to help us increase our listening ability in English. Becoming more aware of the different types of intonation patterns, choices of vocabulary, and styles of communication can help us improve our speaking skills as well.

We will hear a lot of contemporary American slang words on TV. To learn and understand the slang words is one thing; to use them correctly and appropriately is another. We will learn all of the slang and idiomatic expressions we want if we concentrate on that while watching TV. Spending time with your TV can help you improve your English at a fast pace.

Another important use of the TV is keeping up on current events. The TV networks are very good about bringing us the latest news pictures by satellite from around the world. I recommend that you spend time each day watching news programs on TV since you not only broaden your understanding of national and international events and personalities, but also gain valuable, new insights into how Americans view the world. In addition, the cultural gap between you and your American friends will be narrowed because you will be able to discuss topics from current events to the latest weather forecast, from the latest sports results to the latest fads in fashion. Check your local TV guide for the news programs in your area. Better still, ask your friends which programs they prefer to watch and why.

Another valuable aspect of TV is the commercials. You're probably wondering why anyone would recommend commercials. First of all, they can help you when you shop for new products...if you do not blindly believe what you see and hear, but take it all with a grain of salt. Most of these commercials have a clever way of creating needs in their viewers, so be on your guard. Some commercials even exaggerate or misinform the viewers in order to get them to buy their products. Although it's easy to get tricked into buying something which we don't really need or want, the commecials serve us well. In addition to letting us know what the latest products are, they teach us what

Americans value and what motivates them to buy the products and services that they do.

Commercials aren't the only part of TV that can teach us what Americans are like. American movies, dramatic and comic serials, soap operas and talk shows reveal aspects of American life too. We can learn about American values and goals, tastes and desires, heroes and heroines. Foreigners can conveniently learn about American culture from the screen by carefully observing what the characters say and how they act. Sometimes these programs also misinform us and give us incorrect and harmful impressions of Americans. For example, many of the programs emphasize sex and violence . . . yet Americans are not all sex-crazed or criminals. We should carefully pick the programs we are going to watch because too much violence and crime can upset us and cause us to become unduly fearful.

So far I've been discussing the television from a very serious and practical point of view. American TV programs and movies can also help us relax and enjoy ourselves. We can use it as inexpensive entertainment. We can refresh our minds after long periods of intensive study. But don't let it become a crutch. It has adversely affected the reading ability of many American children today because they have spent too many hours passively watching TV programs of little or no value.

As you can see, American TV has both negative aspects and positive ones. If you use your television wisely, you can gain from the positive aspects and avoid the negative. Here's a positive aspect which I haven't mentioned yet. Do you miss your country? In the United States, there are regular TV channels that transmit such foreign language programs as news events, movies, and talk shows. I have seen programming in Mandarin and Cantonese Chinese, Korean, Japanese, Spanish, and Persian. Then, too, there are movies in French, Italian, Swedish, and German. For times and channels, consult your TV guide.

Many of these programs are found on something called cable TV. Recently, cable TV has become very popular here. The cable channels do not have any commercials, so that audiences can watch their programs without interruption. In addition, there are more channels to choose from, and generally these provide programs of better quality, such as current movies and musical specials. Your TV reception is often better too.

In order to have cable TV, you have to order or subscribe to it and pay a monthly fee. To subscribe, you should first find out which companies service your area; often there is only one that is authorized in any given area. The "Television — Cable" section in the Yellow Pages of the telephone book will give you the information on the companies in your area. Simply call a cable company, ask them what their fees are, and then make your decision.

Whatever you decide to watch . . . regular TV or cable TV . . . you have many hours of inexpensive language and cultural training ahead of you, as well as enjoyable, inexpensive entertainment. Keep that TV guide of yours handy at all times!

UNDERSTANDING THE AMERICAN MEASURING SYSTEM

Thomas K. C. Yuan
Hong Kong

Some of us from other countries of the world still view the United States as top contender for the title of "most advanced nation." Even when we disagree with American politics and foreign policies, we still admire her achievements in science and technology, business and economics, education, and the mass media. Indeed, most of us would agree that the United States stands head and shoulders above most other nations.

Being such a forward-thinking and forward-moving nation, the United States ironically continues to use an archaic, illogical measuring system in this predominantly metric world of ours. Such a paradox simply does not "measure up" to what we would expect of this country. Inches, feet, yards, and miles...ounces and pounds...teaspoons, tablespoons, cups, pints, quarts, and gallons...what is the logic behind these units and divisions?

Americans can't seem to offer any explanation, nor can they shed much light on the origins of their measuring system, the rationale behind their not converting to the metric system, or the differences between the two measuring systems. What they can tell you is that, if you plan to spend much time here in the States, you'd better learn their measuring system. You'll need it while shopping at the supermarket, listening to the weather forecast, and traveling around the United States.

Discovering a Little Historical Background

Before we get involved in the "real science" of measurements, let's do a little historical research. Measurements have played an important part in all cultures throughout history. They have been the norms by which traders exchanged goods and services years ago just as today's business people do. Yet often each country has had its own system and has needed a conversion system when it traded with countries having different systems.

A standardized set of measurements was the best solution. This was to come in the form of the so-called metric system (the International System of Units), a decimal system of weights and measures. First used in France in 1799, the metric system quickly spread to most countries of the world, from the European continent to Asia, Africa, Australia, and Latin America. Although some countries were somewhat slow to convert to this system, the United States has been one of the slowest. Today she remains "unmetrically" alone among the important trading nations of the world.

The earliest roots of the American measuring system (The U.S. Customary System of Measurements) can be traced back to the ancient Egyptians whose linear measurement, the *cubit*, was equal in length to a man's forearm. The Greeks later changed *cubit* to *foot* which, according to legend was the actual measurement of the foot of Hercules, the mythological figure credited with founding the Olympic Games. The *foot*, in turn, was adopted by the Romans, who added the *inch* and the *mile*.

As Roman legions marched through Europe, these measurements influenced the people of the areas that they passed through, including Britain. After the fall of the Roman Empire, the Anglo Saxon tribes preserved the *inch*, the *foot*, and the *mile* and introduced the *gird*, said to be the length of their king's belt. King Henry I, a medieval English king, eventually replaced the *gird* with the *yard*, the distance from the tip of his nose to the end of his thumb, but kept the other measurements.

King Henry I would be pleased to know how much of an impact he has had on the United States. If only he could see how many yardsticks are in use here! Yardsticks measure just about anything that is linear and are one yard in length. That means three feet...or 36 inches. How did the Americans end up with these measurements? In much the same way that the Romans brought their measurement concepts to the British Isles, the English brought theirs, along with a language and customs, to America in the 17th century. All of these—language, customs, and measuring system— continue to be part of America's present. The measuring system includes not only those linear measurements already mentioned but additional ones as well as measurements of weight, volume, and temperature.

Converting to the Metric System: Advantages and Disadvantages

You must be wondering what it would take for Americans to convert to the metric system. Even though numerous cases exist throughout American history of both individual and governmental efforts toward change, traditions die hard. For example, a local gas station owner who had converted his pumps to liters is now converting them back to gallons because he found that liters were costing him time, money, and patience; many of his customers continued to insist on purchase amounts in gallons, not liters. Then, too, highway departments of various states have installed signs in both miles and kilometers on some major highways. While this has pleased foreign visitors and immigrants, some Americans complain that it's wasting taxpayers' money. Americans, for the most part, continue to think in miles, not kilometers.

Americans who know the metric system, however, remark on its advantages over the American system. First, it is a scientific system of measurements that is very easy to use. Because its decimal division simplifies all calculations, even someone with a limited amount of mathematical background can easily apply this system to the needs of everyday life. Second, the metric system is used in international trade and commerce.

Converting to the metric system would certainly benefit the American economy by further facilitating trade with other nations. Most American scientists, engineers, and international businessmen acknowledge this and are proponents of a conversion to metric. In fact, some American businesses, such as pharmaceutical firms, are now completely metric, and special groups, such as the American military, are largely metric.

Yet most Americans don't understand the metric system, let alone how to use it. As a result, resistance to change continues to be strong. Even if they could get around the natural aversion to change, the cost of conversion would be very high. Tools, books, signs, and everyday goods would all have to be changed over. Can you imagine the time, effort, and money that it would cost American publishing houses, bookstores, and libraries to convert all printed material to metric? Or how about American households? They would need new measuring devices, new cookbooks, *and* new housewives! Who could pay that high a price?

Asking Americans to change their measuring system would be a little bit like asking the Chinese to write all of their books in the **pinyin** phonetic alphabet instead of the Chinese characters that they are used to. Even literary tradition would be challenged! Can you imagine changing the lines of this Robert Frost poem to read *kilometers* instead of *miles?*

> *"The woods are lovely, dark, and deep,*
> *But I have promises to keep,*
> *And miles to go before I sleep,*
> *And miles to go before I sleep."*

Comparing the Metric and American Measuring Systems

To have a better idea of how the American Measuring System differs from the metric, try this one on for size! There are 63,360 inches, 5280 feet, and 1760 yards in a mile. Even though all Americans commonly use these four units, most could not have given you this information without consulting a table.

We can draw a number of conclusions from this little discussion. First, the relationships between units in the American measuring system seem random and illogical, whereas the relationships between units in the metric system are completely logical. Metric system units are based on "the powers of 10"; quantities greater than the base are indicated by Greek prefixes, such as *deka-*, *hecto-* and *kilo-*, whereas quantities less than the base are indicated by Latin prefixes, such as *deci-*, *centi-*, and *milli-*.

Second, there are fewer unit names in the metric system than in the American measuring system. Whereas the American measuring system uses distinct names for all units within each of the main measurement categories, the metric system uses only one. *Meter* is used for measures of length and area, *gram* for measures of mass (weight), and *liter* for measures of volume.

Using the American Measuring System

It should now be clear that while you are in the United States, at least in the present and near future, you will be using the American measuring system. The sooner you get busy with a conversion table and learn the more commonly used measures, the more comfortable, confident, and competent you will feel. If you do any food shopping or cooking, you'll need to convert grams and kilograms to ounces and pounds; liters to pints, quarts, and gallons. If you buy fabric for a dress or lumber for a fence, you'll have to convert meters to yards, feet, and inches. Finally, if you want to know how to dress for the weather, you'll have to convert Centigrade to Fahrenheit!

Where can you find a chart with the basic conversions? If you don't already have a conversion chart, a handy and inexpensive one can be obtained by going to the nearest U.S. Government Bookstore or by writing to the following address:

Superintendent of Documents
U.S. Government Printing Office
Washington, D.C. 20402

 # METRIC CONVERSION CHART

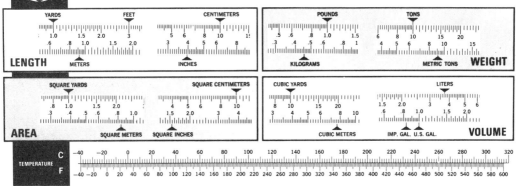

CHAPTER 3
FINDING YOUR
WAY AROUND

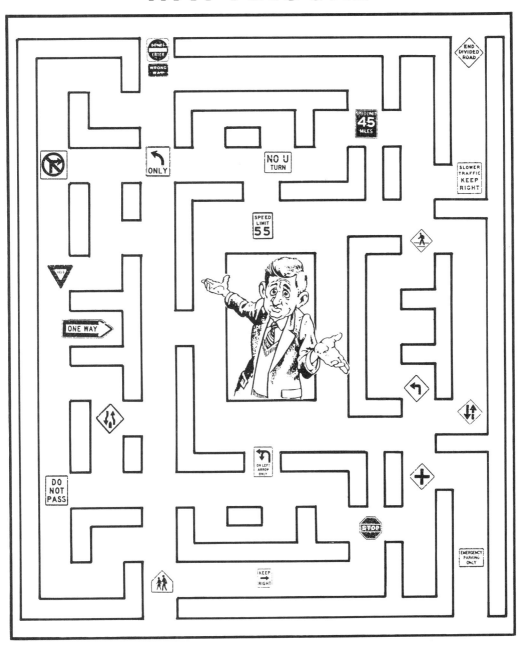

3. INTRODUCTION

Whether you plan to remain in the United States for a short visit or for an extended stay, you will need to find your way around in order to accomplish a number of important tasks. You will have to walk, ride a bike, take a bus, or drive a car in order to obtain a driver's license, buy groceries, get a check cashed, or mail a letter. Making a conscious effort to find your way around your new community in order to take advantage of the services, institutions, and entertainment available to you will help you feel more confident, productive, and at home here.

The first four articles in this chapter will help you understand your local bus system, as well as the steps you need to follow if you decide to buy a car and get a driver's license. Generally, a car is more convenient to use in the United States than public transportation, especially in such cities as Los Angeles and Phoenix. However, there are exceptions. In San Francisco, for example, it is probably more convenient . . . and fun . . . to use public transportation than to use a car. Once you have decided what form of transportation to use, you will be able to make good use of the information in the final three articles in this chapter: using a bank, a post office, and supermarket.

UNDERSTANDING THE LOCAL BUS SYSTEM

Badlin Fung
Taiwan

Few foreign students are fortunate enough to find housing close to their colleges and universities. Many of those living at a distance from school will not have access to a car or motorcycle. Therefore, they will have to rely on public transportation . . . the bus.

If you decide to ride a bus, find out what bus company is responsible for public transportation in your area. Get its phone number and be prepared to use it in order to get the information you will need.

In a recent survey of foreign students who ride the bus to school, it was found that four questions predominate. First of all, how should a foreign student choose the correct bus to take, and when and where should he transfer to another? Secondly, when does the bus pass by a certain spot? Third, how much will it cost to ride the bus, and are there student passes available? Fourth, what are the procedures for getting on and off buses, paying the fares, and getting transfers?

Getting the right answers to these questions will help you to understand the local bus system, to save time, and to avoid the frustration of making mistakes. Understanding the local bus system is not an official part of your academic curriculum; however, it is an invaluable asset, especially if, like me, you need to rely on public transportation during your academic life in the United States.

Note: When paying fares, some bus services require exact change, others allow drivers to make change—rules may vary in different cities.

BUYING A CAR

Ching-Yung Ni
People's Republic of China

Some metropolitan areas lack an accessible and convenient public transportation system. Living in an area without adequate public transportation may necessitate having a car of your own, especially if you live at some distance from school or work. If you should decide to buy a car, you should consider some important matters before deciding on a purchase.

Deciding on the Car

Financial considerations are often the most crucial ones since they will often determine whether you buy or lease either a new or used car, whether you pay cash or make payments, and whether you decide on an economy car or a sports model. How much money are you willing or able to spend on the initial cost of the car, on monthly payments, and on the cost of regular auto maintenance as well as on unexpected mechanical failures? The size and fuel efficiency of the car are two other factors which involve your finances, for they will determine consequent fuel expenses. Consider, too, how many passengers you will most often be taking with you. This will also help determine the size of the car you will buy.

When you choose a car, remember that the cost of insurance is higher on sports cars. If possible, ask the opinions of people who have owned a car like the one that you want. You might also consider the resale value of the car if you plan to sell it back within a few years. You will, of course, be better off with a car that maintains its value. Imported cars usually have better resale values than American cars, although their initial costs are often greater.

Once you have decided what kind of car you want, you have to choose between a manual or an automatic transmission. A manual transmission usually involves fewer mechanical problems than an automatic, while the automatic transmission is often more convenient. Then, too, what color exterior and interior do you prefer? What optional equipment and accessories do you wish? An air conditioning system, a stereo radio and tape deck, and a luggage rack all add to the cost of the car.

Making the Purchase

When you have in mind exactly what car you would like to have, find out where you can get the lowest possible prices on the car. Also, compare the prices at various dealerships. Discuss the prices with each salesperson in order to bring your final price down.

Once you have found the best deal, you are ready to buy your car or place an order for it. If you are not going to pay cash for your car but are going to finance it, a down payment of about 20% of the purchase price is usually required. Finding the right financing is the important next step.

Financing the Car

Although the dealer will probably offer you a financing plan, you might be better off to investigate what kinds of financing you can arrange yourself through a financial institution, such as a bank or savings and loan. The dealer will be going through a bank anyway and may be adding several percentage points to the interest rate for his own profit.

So, shop around for the bank that offers the most convenient interest rate. Once you have decided where to finance your car, take the purchase order to them for processing. As soon as the loan is approved, you can pick up your car. Now it's yours to drive and enjoy . . . except for those payments which are due every month.

Note: See Article 9.3, pp. 136–137, for further suggestions on buying new and used cars.

GETTING A DRIVER'S LICENSE

Sheng-Cheng Koo
Taiwan
and
Agus Supriadi
Indonesia

When I first came to the United States, two of my friends took me around in their cars almost every day during the month before school started. We went to the movies, the beaches, and to such local attractions as Disneyland, Universal Studios, and Sea World. When school started the following month, however, my friends became very busy, and I knew a profound loneliness for the first time in my life. I spent my time reading newspapers or watching television. I began to feel bored and frustrated.

When I wanted to go out to a movie or a party, the same problems always faced me. How could I get there? I couldn't do it on foot. When I wanted to cook and was out of ingredients, I had to go to a supermarket. Again I faced the same problem. How could I get to a supermarket if the closest one was five miles from where I lived? The day I wanted to attend the orientation program at school, I took the bus and had to change buses three times. It took me more than an hour of travel time.

Now I drive my own car and feel that I am my own man. Because of a car, I get my studying and food shopping done and still have time for fun. The same type of experience has occurred, and will continue to occur, for many foreign students who come to the United States for the first time. It should be obvious that driving a car and having a driver's license here are of utmost importance!

Why We Need a Driver's License

Transportation — Nowadays, the most common form of transportation in the United States is the car. Every day, we can see hundreds of thousands of cars pass on streets, roads, and freeways. In fact, the car has become an integral part of American life. Sometimes we can't separate the car from the American! Why has the car become so important here?

First, distances between places are often so great that it is almost impossible to get everywhere on foot. Second, there is very little efficient and adequate public transportation here. Buses, trains, and taxis are not so plentiful as in other parts of the world. Third, it is very inconvenient to travel by public transportation. When we want to travel by bus, for example, we have to walk to the bus stop and wait for the bus. Also, we frequently have to change buses to get to where we're going. If we go by car, however, we don't have to go through all of this. We just get into the car and start the engine, and within a few minutes we are already at our destination. Fourth, by driving a car, not only do we save time, but we also have more freedom and independence.

Finally, some Americans might even say that a car is an extension of their homes because they spend so much of their lives in them. Let me tell you one thing which shows how crazy Americans are about cars. In a recent survey at my college, most people responded with an overwhelming "yes" to the question: "Do you need a car?" They gave the following reasons for the necessity of having a car: "It's easier to get around; it's more comfortable; you can't depend on the bus." One American even said he might consider living in his car if rents went much higher! Those who didn't own cars said that they didn't only because cars were too expensive for limited student budgets. Most people believe that a car is almost indispensable here.

Identification — If we do not have a car, however, we should still consider having a driver's license. It often functions as an identification card ("I.D."). For example, if we buy something and want to pay for it by check, we are often asked to show our driver's license in addition to a credit card. Again, if we want to open an account in a bank, we will often be asked to show our driver's license as I.D. Finally, if we want to have an alcoholic beverage in a public place, we may be asked to show our I.D. as proof that we meet the age requirement.

How to Get a Driver's License

Since we know that having a driver's license brings us many advantages, it would be foolish for us not to try to get one. But how can we get a driver's license? Don't worry! A driver's license is not something special. Everyone can get one because it's not costly or difficult to obtain. To get a driver's license, you should first go to the nearest Department of Motor Vehicles (D.M.V.) with your passport or your birth certificate. There, you will pick up an application form which you will fill out. If there is something that you don't understand, you can ask the person at the information desk or other people who are filling out their application forms.

After completing the application form, take it to the registration window. You'll have to pay a small fee and show your passport or birth certificate to the person at the window. After he finishes checking your documents, he will take your money and give you a receipt along with a printed test paper. If you are not ready to take the test, you can take it later when you are ready.

"But how can I pass the test?" you ask. "I don't even know the traffic regulations here." It's true that most foreign students who take the test without any preparation fail it. The reason is that traffic regulations in the U.S.A. are somewhat different from those in other countries. How do you prepare yourself for such a test? Just ask for a "Driver's Handbook" from the D.M.V. and study it. If your English is not quite strong enough yet to do the test preparation and test-taking in English, just ask if they have the booklet in your own language. In some states there are copies of it in quite a few languages, such as Spanish, Japanese, and Korean. All the material which will show up on the test is in that handbook. So, if you have learned the handbook, you are sure to pass the test.

When you are ready, go back to the D.M.V. and take the written test. The test consists of 36 multiple choice questions. Here are four typical exam questions:

1. The proper hand-arm signal for a right turn is:
   a. Arm held straight in horizontal position.
   b. Arm bent at elbow, hand pointing up.
   c. Arm held down, hand pointing at ground.
2. When two cars reach a corner from different streets at the same time, the legal right of way belongs to:
   a. The car on the right.
   b. The car on the left.
   c. The car moving fastest.
3. Throwing bottles, cans, paper, or anything from your window is:
   a. Forbidden only inside city limit.
   b. Forbidden only outside city limit.
   c. Forbidden at all times.
4. The speed limit when you come within 100 ft. of a railroad crossing where you cannot see the tracks for 400 ft. in both directions is:
   a. 10 M.P.H.
   b. 15 M.P.H.
   c. 25 M.P.H.

There is no time limit for taking this test, so you don't have to hurry. Maybe you'll feel a little nervous, as I did when I took the test. If you do, just take a deep breath, and everything will be all right.

After you finish the written test, take it to the correction window. Again, if you don't know where the window is, don't be ashamed to ask somebody. The person at that window will correct your work. The maximum number you may miss and still pass the test is 5. If you make more than 5 mistakes, you have failed the test. But don't worry; even if you fail, you still have two more chances to take the test without having to pay the fee again. If you pass the test, you will be given an eye test which asks you to read a chart of letters which vary in size and are posted about 3 meters (10 feet) away. This test will determine whether your vision is safe for the road. After that, the person at the window will give you a temporary license. With this type of license, you are allowed to drive a car during the daylight as long as there is somebody who has a driver's license sitting beside you. This temporary license will expire one year from the date it is given. So, during this period, you should take the road test in order to get a permanent license.

Take the road test as soon as you feel comfortable with the driving conditions here.

To take the road test, you may have to make an appointment first. On the appointed day and hour, you should be at the D.M.V. on time. During the road test, which is about 15 minutes long, the examiner will test your general driving skills: starting your vehicle, leaving a parking place, giving signals, parallel parking, backing up, changing lanes, turning around, and changing directions. Whatever you do, listen carefully to your examiner. Remember always to follow precautionary procedures before following his instructions.

After you have done all these things, he will ask you to drive back to the D.M.V. The road test is over now, and he will give you your score. The minimum score for passing is 75%. If you pass, take your test results to the photograph window. The person at that window will give you a license which is valid for 60 days. After that, he will take your picture for your permanent license, which will be mailed to your address.

When you have a license and can drive a car by yourself, you'll see how much easier your life becomes. You'll be able to get places quickly, save time and energy, and acquire greater freedom and independence. Not only that, you will now have the perfect I.D. for all situations!

Note: Because rules and regulations on how to get a driver's license tend to vary slightly from one state to another, check with your local agency that issues driver's licenses about the procedures for your state. The name of this agency also varies from state to state. In California and New York, for example, this agency is called the Department of Motor Vehicles, commonly referred to as D.M.V., while in Texas it is called the Department of Public Safety, commonly referred to as D.P.S.

BUYING AUTO INSURANCE

Franky Lengkong
Indonesia

Automobile insurance is necessary for people who intend to drive in the United States. It is now mandatory in certain states such as California. How do you find the right insurance for you? How much will you have to pay?

When looking for insurance, you will find that rates vary according to the coverage that you desire, your age and sex, the area that you live in, the distance and type of car that you drive, and your driving record. If you are an unmarried male, under the age of 25 who drives a new car, lives in an accident-prone area, and needs the car for long distance driving on a daily basis, an insurance company will charge you a much higher rate. If you are a married male over 25 years of age, have a car with a low market value, and live in a quiet community, a company will charge you a lower rate.

The reasons for this should be obvious. Unmarried male drivers under age 25 tend to have the highest number of accidents. They are considered less experienced and less responsible than those who are older and have a wife and family. And, if the driver travels long distances on a daily basis, the chances of being in an accident are much higher than for someone who drives short distances only occasionally.

There are two basic types of automobile insurance. One is called collision insurance (comprehensive or full coverage insurance), and the other is called liability insurance. Under collision or full coverage insurance, if you have an accident and it is your fault, your insurance company will take care of all expenses except the deductible which you pay (usually $100-$1000). These expenses include all injuries suffered by the other person and damage done to his vehicle as well as those injuries suffered by you and damage done to your car.

The second category of car insurance is called liability insurance. It is compulsory in some states for a driver or owner of a vehicle at least to have liability insurance. Basically, liability insurance protects only the driver of the other car in case of an accident. It pays for the damages done to another driver if you are found responsible for an accident, but it does not cover damages to you or your car. Liability insurance costs much less than comprehensive collision insurance, but the coverage is limited. In the opinion of most experts, comprehensive insurance coverage is the kind of insurance you should have if you can afford it. Depending on the value of your car, it is worth the extra cost, especially if you are ever involved in a car accident. A good insurance company to get information from about your various options is the Automobile Club of America (AAA). This involves no obligation on your part. With the information from AAA, you can then look into what other insurance companies have to offer.

It is important to have exactly the amount of coverage that you need and no more. Some people are insurance poor. That is, they have spent so much money on insurance that they don't have money for other expenditures. You need to buy only the amount of coverage that is necessary to protect you and your family from unexpected costs from an auto accident or theft.

Note: The American Automobile Association (AAA) is often referred to as Triple A. However, its regional affiliates sometimes have slightly different names. Call the telephone operator for the correct name and phone number. In addition, other companies such as the National Automobile Club, offer automobile services also.

USING A BANK

Kathrine Tabibzadeh
Greece/Iran

The American banking system is the most complex banking system that I have seen anywhere in the world. It consists of many different types of accounts, ranging from checking accounts to saving accounts, business accounts to T-bill accounts. There is also a type of banking system known as the savings and loan, where you can save money for long periods of time and earn greater interest. What banking services might be of interest to foreign students? How do we take advantage of these services? How do we open an account?

If you would like to open an account, find a bank close to the place where you live or work. Find out the banking hours and go early or when few people are there so that you can get better service and don't have to stand in long lines. Go to a desk marked "New Accounts" and ask for information. It is a good idea to have with you an official I.D. or a valid driver's license, a passport, a credit card if you have one, or even a birth certificate. At least two of these forms of identification are normally required.

After you have enough information about services available, choose the account or accounts best for you.

The Savings Account

The savings account is one of the best known and most useful services of a bank. It allows you to keep your money in a safe place and earn interest at the same time. Almost everything is done by computer which cuts down on errors. Therefore, you can feel assured that your money will be handled safely.

A savings account is one which allows you to add or withdraw money merely by presenting a passbook in which your deposits and withdrawals are recorded. You need to learn how to use two forms. One is called a deposit slip, which you fill out when you put money into your account. This is a typical example of a savings deposit slip:

SAVINGS ACCOUNT
DEPOSIT TICKET

ACCOUNT CARRIED AT

OFFICE NO   ACCOUNT NO

NAME

DATE _____

LIST CHECKS BY BANK NUMBER		DOLLARS	CENTS
CURRENCY			
COIN			
CHECKS 1			
2			
3			
4			
5			
6			
7			
8			
FOR TELLER	TOTAL DEPOSIT		

The other is called a withdrawal slip, which you fill out when you take money out of your account. Here is an example of a typical savings withdrawal slip:

SAVINGS ACCOUNT WITHDRAWAL TICKET

	DATE _____

ACCOUNT CARRIED AT	OFFICE NO.	ACCOUNT NO.

RECEIVED FROM $ _____

_____ DOLLARS

SIGNATURE _____

FOR TELLER	ADDRESS _____
$	_____

15Y 100 (3) 5-84 030270

The Checking Account

A second type of account is the checking account; it is useful in a number of ways.

1. If you have a checking account, you do not need to have cash, for you can buy the things that you need and pay your bills without ever leaving home!

2. Most banks will send you all cancelled checks each month; these serve as proof that you have made a payment on a bill or debt.

3. The statement of your account, which you receive at the end of the month, shows all deposits and withdrawals. Keep these statements safe. They allow you to verify your own records with those of the bank concerning the amount of money in your account.

Most banks charge a small amount of money each month on checking accounts which have less than a certain amount in them or accounts on which more than a certain numbers of checks have been drawn. Other banks charge a fee for each check written. These are charges which help pay the bank's expenses. Be sure that you know what the policies of your bank are.

This is an example of a check, properly filled out.

May 1, 19 55   16-4/1220

PAY TO THE ORDER OF _J. L. Mosley Management_ $ 100⁰⁰

One hundred and no/100s DOLLARS

FOR _____   Ling Ling Co

⑆ 1220000431⑆0222⑈ 248⑈043114⑈

51

The Credit Card

Finally, an important service of any bank is its international credit card. In order to get a credit card, you need to have an account at the bank. The credit card is used when you don't have money with you; it can, therefore, be very convenient. Credit cards are useful for I.D., and are sometimes required by stores in order to pay with a check. Of course, most banks require proof that you receive a certain amount of money each month, either from a job or from your family.

These are only three of the many services that banks offer: a safe place to keep your money while accumulating interest, a means of writing checks, and the use of a credit card. They certainly are valuable services to take advantage of and will make your life here easier and more convenient!

USING THE POST OFFICE

Kathrine Tabibzadeh
Greece/Iran

If it is as important for you to communicate with your friends and relatives as it is for me, you will want to learn the basic procedures of the United States Post Office.

How the Post Office Operates

The Post Office is a place where mail is handled and postage stamps are sold. Through the Post Office, you can do virtually everything from paying bills to buying items through mail order services. Using the postal system in America is much easier to figure out than in many other countries. In my country, for example, every time you send a letter, the cost of postage is different. Here in the United States, if you are mailing a basic letter, it costs 22 cents no matter to what city or state the letter is being sent. Mailing outside the United States costs 44 cents per letter, except to Mexico and Canada where the cost is the same as within the United States.

The Post Office is generally open during regular business hours. There is also a place in most Post Offices where you can mail letters and buy stamps from a machine twenty-four hours a day.

What Services the Post Office Offers

Here are some of the services that are offered at the Post Office, other than mailing letters:

1. **Postage Stamps.** The Post Office sells postage stamps to put on letters or packages. Their stamps are proof that the sender has paid for sending his mail.
2. **Stamped Envelopes and Aerograms.** The Post Office also sells envelopes with postage printed on them for domestic mail and aerograms, lightweight fold-up letters with postage printed on them, for international air mail. Aerograms save about 8 cents per letter abroad.
3. **Post Cards.** These are sold by the Post Office and have the postage printed on them but cost only the value of the postage. Private companies make post cards, but these cards do not have stamps on them and often have pictures and less space for a message.
4. **P.O. Boxes.** These are locked boxes which may be rented in Post Offices as a place to receive mail. Individuals and companies often use them because they provide fast and convenient mail delivery. Mail can be collected even after regular Post Office hours.
5. **Certified Mail.** If a person wants proof that he mailed a letter or package, he can

pay a small fee at the time of mailing. All he needs to do is to fill out a form which the Post Office then certifies as legal proof that he mailed the letter or package.

6. **Express Mail.** This service provides overnight delivery of letters or packages up to 70 pounds with a money-back guarantee, within the downtown areas of more than 400 American cities. Major cities abroad can be reached in two or three days.

7. **Money Orders.** Post Offices sell money orders to provide a safe and convenient way to send money through the mail.

8. **Other Services.** The Post Office also serves as the headquarters for the registration of aliens. Some also accept passport applications, give information regarding Civil Service employment, and furnish national and state tax forms. If you move, you should fill out a change of address form; your mail will then be forwarded to your new address. Likewise, if you have a small mailbox and plan to be away from home for a week or more, you should fill out a form to have your mail held at your local Post Office until you return. Then your mailbox will not be overflowing with mail during your absence. For more information, call your local Post Office.

Why the Post Office Is Important to You

The Post Office provides an inexpensive way to communicate with your family and friends, as well as to pay bills and get public information. Many business and social transactions are carried on by mail. Remember the motto of the Post Office: "Neither snow, nor rain, nor heat, nor gloom of night, keeps these couriers from the swift completion of their appointed rounds." You can always count on the Post Office to come through.

SHOPPING IN A SUPERMARKET

Silvia-Tamira Powell
Brazil

I don't remember spending as much time in supermarkets in my native country as I am doing now in the U.S. The American supermarket is a place which can supply us with foods and beverages; cleaning, health, and beauty aids; stationery, plants, and flowers; china, glassware, pots, pans, and utensils; clothing; fishing and camping equipment; magazines and books; and a most extensive variety of pet foods.

The first time I went to a supermarket in the United States, I found myself surrounded by fresh, frozen, and canned foods, most of which were unfamiliar to me. I was unable to find familiar spices, baking supplies, and foods. The variety of cleaning aids was confusing, and the large section for pets was perplexing! After many trips to the supermarket, I began to focus on exactly what I needed to buy.

In the process, I learned the importance of reading product labels. Since most of us are going to buy American products for the first time, it is a good idea to *read the labels of food and beverage packages* for nutritional information, not to mention the directions and warnings on cleaning and health-aid bottles and containers. If we do this before we buy, we will save ourselves a lot of time and trouble in the long run.

Looking for label information is not the only thing that we have to keep in mind. We might as well think about saving money, too. There are three ways to save money in a supermarket. The first is done by looking for products which are on sale or offered at lower-than-normal prices. Another way is by using manufacturers' *coupons* in conjunction with the double and triple supermarket discount coupons. A manufacturer's coupon of 10 cents would be worth 20 cents when used with a store's double coupon, and 30 cents when used with a store's triple coupon. These coupons are usually found in newspapers once or twice a week. A third way to save money is by *checking the prices in special advertisements*. You may learn of these items through radio and TV advertisements or special fliers distributed in stores, sent through the mail, or delivered door-to-door. Sometimes these fliers are inserted in daily newspapers, too.

In addition to saving money, we can also *save time*. If we have only a few items to buy and are able to pay cash, we may save time by using the *express lanes*. To make check cashing easier, many supermarkets have *courtesy cards* for which customers may apply. These cards enable us to pay for groceries with a check and, in some cases, to cash personal checks for small amounts over the price of our purchase.

The American supermarket is a part of everyday life in America. Knowing exactly what to buy and what is available, and how to save time and money, should be of help to anyone who is living on his own for the first time in the United States. Even though all of this is new to you, enjoy the adventure ahead!

CHAPTER 4
GETTING TO KNOW AMERICANS

4. INTRODUCTION

"When you leave a country, you leave behind something of your heart," *says a Belgian proverb. You no doubt agree, for you have probably already experienced a certain longing for family and friends left behind in your home country. Yet here you will have many opportunities to make new friendships, not to replace the old familiar ones, but to make your life more enjoyable and meaningful while you are here, and to enrich your life forever.*

All around you are strangers whom you haven't met yet, but who are potential friends. Without friends, your American experience will offer little to enrich your humanity, your understanding, and your heart. As Robert Louis Stevenson, the Scottish poet and novelist, once said: "A friend is a present that you give yourself . . . for friends are the end and reward of life . . ."

Plan on making the effort to make some new friends, and let some of that effort be spent on Americans. You and they have much to learn from each other. A word of caution, however. People from different cultures do not always have the same attitudes toward friendship. As you enter into a relationship with an American or someone of a different culture, keep an open mind and a tolerant attitude when someone doesn't treat you the way that you expect.

The articles in this chapter will set you in the right direction by suggesting how to make friends with Americans, how to date them, and how to give gifts the American way.

MAKING FRIENDS WITH AMERICANS

Delmy Cornejo
El Salvador

When I first set foot on American soil over half a decade ago, I posed these questions to myself: What are Americans really like? Are they friendly and kind to foreigners or are they prejudiced against them? Will they be easy to get to know and make friends with?

I was too young then to discern the truth about Americans or completely understand their way of life. Even though I was naive and half-scared, I was determined to keep an open mind and an open heart, and to make every effort to meet and get to know them. It was the best decision I could have made under the circumstances. My parents had decided to move to the United States; it was to be our new home.

In the process of adjustment to American life, I took each day as it came. Some days were difficult; others were easy. I can now say that I have accomplished something truly wonderful. I have become comfortable here and have made many new friends.

Whether you make this country your new home, or whether you eventually return to your native country, you should consider some of the methods and techniques that I have learned for making friends with Americans. Acquiring friends in the United States will help you feel at home here as I do. Try to make friends using these techniques at every opportunity.

First, drop your negative judgments about how different things are compared to the way they are in your country. As long as they don't conflict with your own values, be willing to adopt those American customs and traditions which in your judgment are acceptable, perhaps even valuable.

Second, work on your language and communication skills. Speak slowly, clearly, and loudly enough to communicate your views or ideas effectively. Many foreigners tend to speak too quietly. Practice pronunciation exercises daily in order to sound more native. If someone does not understand you the first time, be ready to repeat your request or point of view. Listening well is another part of the communication process. Make sure that you have listened and understood what someone has said to you.

Third, convince Americans that you want to meet them and get to know them. Here are some ways to be convincing:

1. Join a club at school or participate in a sport. One of the best clubs on my campus is the International Club. This club brings you into contact with Americans who tend to be interested in foreign students, foreign cultures, and foreign languages. So your chances of meeting some Americans that you will hit it off with are excellent.

2. Join clubs and organizations outside school, such as the Y.M.C.A., the Y.W.C.A., or

other health clubs, religious organizations, and community organizations. These associations will help keep you healthy and involved while exposing you to Americans, American English in authentic situations, and American life styles.

3. Demonstrate your skills and talents by volunteering in areas where you can prove that you are an asset! What are your strengths and abilities? Put them to good use in some worthwhile activity or organization. See how people begin to include you.

4. A smile will do more than almost anything to melt away interpersonal and intercultural barriers. So, smile, smile, smile! Nothing will draw people to you quicker than a friendly smile!

5. Be yourself. Act casually and naturally so as not to create the impression of being hypocritical or superficial. The *real* you is what will appeal to others.

Some of you may be asking yourselves why you should make such an effort to get to know Americans and make some American friends. There are many advantages in doing so. You will increase your self-confidence, which will help you in your studies, your future career, and in many other areas of your life. You will increase your understanding of your own culture in addition to understanding American culture better. By making American friends you will adjust more quickly to your new environment; adequate adjustment will help you feel comfortable and at home. You will improve your English communication skills; your pronunciation will become increasingly more acceptable, your understanding of current idiomatic expressions will be enhanced, and your use of correct American English will become second nature. You will gain a larger perspective; you will realize that race, color, and language need not be barriers when communicating with other human beings.

You may be worried that you might become too Americanized and forget who you are and where you came from. That is something that you may always need to guard against. Over-Americanization depletes you, for it leaves you with no roots. In the process, you could become an "outcast" among your own people, as well as to yourself. You must always ask, "Who am I?" and never forget the answer or leave yourself behind. Americans who don't want to know the real you and accept you as you are aren't people to cultivate as friends.

I have made many American friends by practicing the procedures mentioned above. As a famous Roman by the name of Cicero once said: "Life is nothing without friendship." Create an American experience for yourself that will be full of meaningful and lasting memories. Make yourself some good American friends!

DATING AMERICANS

Atika D. Adhiningrant
Indonesia
and
Hrant Bedrossian
Iran

Interested in dating Americans? You may not be able to answer that question yet, but you are probably at least interested in the subject. Dating can be a problem for foreign students because of the difference in culture and customs. This article may help you decide whether you are interested in dating Americans, and if you decide that you are, it may help you feel more confident when it comes time for your first date with an American.

First, do not be deceived by what you see in the movies. It may be both partly true and partly false. If American movies tend to make you feel prejudiced against the Americans, you have to remember that those movies are often products of Hollywood. If true at all, they often show only what is superficial and most apparent. From experience, we know that we cannot always judge people by their appearances.

As a new arrival here in the United States, it will take a while for you to learn how people act socially, and how they date. With determination, it will not take long for you to know some Americans well enough to be dating one of them soon, if that's what you'd like to do.

The majority of American college and university students who are in their late teens and early twenties date. If you do find an American who does not date, he probably is engaged or already married.

What is the significance of American dating? Often dating means no more than getting to know one another and having some fun. It is often the beginning of a friendship with someone whom you may like but not necessarily marry. Dating is not as serious in America as it is in some countries, but it is important because every person has the freedom to choose his own marriage partner, one with whom he hopes to spend the rest of his life. Dating is one way to accomplish that goal.

Where do most Americans go on a typical date? A frequent place to go is the movies. After the movie, going out for a bite to eat is usually in order. Finally, the boy takes the girl back home and says good night. That is usually the end of it, at least the first time out with someone.

On a first date, some American women prefer to go "Dutch treat." This means that the girl pays for herself. Because Americans are informal in their dating patterns, there is no rule that says the boy always has to pay. Maybe some of you do not agree with this, but some Americans prefer it. In most foreign countries, the boy usually pays all expenses when he takes a girl out, even on the first date. The girl never pays unless it is a special occasion. Then the girl may insist on paying, but only if they have gone out together for quite a while. This is not necessarily so here.

As a relationship becomes warmer and more intimate, you can guess what subject is likely to come up. If you were thinking about sex, you are correct! There are many different attitudes about how to handle this question, even among Americans. In this area, it is unpredictable how Americans approach the question. Some are liberal, some conservative. Some even say one thing and do another! This is a difficult area even for Americans, because even they cannot always predict how their dates will react to the question of "how far to go" sexually. The best solution is to be honest about what you believe is the limit, and stick to it!

Now, where can you meet people to date? They are almost everywhere: at school, at work, at a club activity, or even at the supermarket. You can be sure you will find someone, unless of course, someone finds you first.

Some Americans have an interest in people from foreign cultures, but many of them don't. Since it's extremely difficult to deal with those who don't, try to focus on the ones who are more inclined to have an interest in you.

I came to the States three years ago from a Middle Eastern country. During my stay, I have had a number of American friends and girl friends. Much of my success came as a result of the extra time and energy I devoted to understanding their culture and social behavior, and overcoming the differences that created obstacles for a relationship. Here are some observations that helped me and may help you.

Observation #1: If you're going to speak, make sure it's English. Because effective communication is the most important aspect of a relationship, you need to learn some English to converse with your date because most Americans don't know any other languages. The better your English, the better you will communicate. The better you communicate, the more chances you have for dating successfully. It is very important to know idioms and some slang, too. They constitute a considerable part of American everyday language.

Observation #2: If you're going to smell, make sure it's sweet! You've probably already discovered that people from different cultures don't always smell the same or appreciate the same smells. The media-conditioned Americans prefer the scents of cosmetic products to the natural smells of the body. Yet is has been scientifically proven that the smell of sweat of a clean body can attract the opposite sex. Many Americans, however, feel the need to cover up natural smells created by the secretion of glands during physical activity with artificial perfumes or colognes. So in order to please most American dates, you have to wear deodorant and an after-shave lotion or perfume at all times! This can be an inconvenience if you are living in the midst of another ethnic group.

Let me tell you of my own experience. When I got together with my family after being in the United States for two years, I was shocked to notice that my father smelled awful. He never had before. A few days later I realized that, like most males in the Middle Eastern countries, he wasn't using deodorant at all. In two years my attitudes toward smell had changed to such an extent that I was bothered by the smell of my own father! As a result, my father began to use deodorant at the age of 72.

Observation #3: If you're unhappy, make sure you have a smile on your face! When your American date asks you, "How are you?" some suggested answers you might give, depending on your mood, are as follows:

If you feel just great, say: "Excellent!"

If you feel good, say: "I'm fine."

If you feel merely okay, say: "I'm just fine."

If you feel awful, say: "I can't complain."

Screen your negative feelings a little up until the time you become intimate friends. Americans have a strong protective shell, but don't worry, they are usually valuable friends.

After all that, do you still want to date Americans? "Yes," you say? Let me give you some good news. Despite all the difficulties mentioned above, once you have started the relationship, it will be very easy for you to keep it going. You are probably much more experienced in maintaining deep and lasting relationships than your American friend is. If you can succeed in bending your way initially (language, cologne, and hidden feelings), you'll be surprised and delighted to find your friend following you in your way a bit later.

So have you finally answered the question? If your answer is yes, have fun, and good luck! If your answer is no, remember to keep making American friends of *both* sexes, just in case you change your mind.

GIVING GIFTS THE AMERICAN WAY

Tri Lam
Viet Nam

Gift giving is a "natural" custom in all countries, but when you move from your home environment to a foreign one, what has been natural and taken for granted can become unnatural and out of place. In the United States, gift giving has a natural set of rules and conventions that may be different from the ones in your country. Foreign students must work to acquire a knowledge of the American gift giving rules and conventions.

Americans tend to be a generous people. They love to give gifts on a number of occasions. These occasions may be similar to or different from the occasions on which foreigners give gifts. Even if the occasion is the same or similar, the kind of gift required and the manner of giving and receiving the gift may be different. Gift giving will require a little thought and consideration; you may need to ask questions or consult an etiquette book when in doubt about a particular gift, such as a shower or wedding gift. For most Americans, the most wonderful and enjoyable time to give a gift is when you merely want to show love, affection, or appreciation to a friend or family member. A gift sometimes shows your warm feelings toward someone more effectively than words. Sometimes a gift is an expression of thanks to someone who has done you a favor or invited you to dinner. At other times, gifts are social obligations which need to be fulfilled graciously.

In this country there are many occasions on which you might want or need to give a gift. Birthdays, weddings, Father's Day, Mother's Day, and Valentine's Day are some of the special days on which to give people a card and gift to show that you remember them. Americans love to be remembered on their birthdays, and most parents are appreciative when their sons and daughters remember them on Mother's and Father's Days, which occur each year in May and June, respectively. Newspaper advertisements and TV commercials will let you know when the day is at hand and will be full of suggestions for what to buy your parent on that special day. On Valentine's Day, which falls on February 14th each year, a box of chocolates or bouquet of flowers and a card with a sentimental but heartfelt verse will make any special someone happy.

Other important gift-giving holidays include Christmas and Easter. Almost any thoughtful gift is appropriate for Christmas, while for Easter, white Easter lilies or cut flowers would be appropriate for adults, and chocolate candies or a stuffed animal are appropriate for children. When you are invited to someone's home for dinner or a party, especially on Christmas or Easter, you might want to bring the hostess a small bouquet of pretty flowers, a box of fine chocolates, or a bottle of good wine.

Another occasion when a gift is a must is a wedding. How much you spend on the wedding gift depends on how close you are to the bride or groom or to one of the family members. You also need to consider your budget when you go shopping for the gift. In some countries, money is an acceptable gift. However, money is usually not considered an appropriate wedding gift here. Sometimes the bride is registered at a department store or a china shop; calling her mother to find out what the bride would really like is always an excellent thing to do. The mother is usually delighted to tell you if her daughter is registered somewhere and what other household items might be needed. A wedding gift can be as practical as a toaster or as impractical as a cut crystal vase. You should usually choose a gift which the new couple can use and enjoy.

If you are a woman, you may even receive an invitation to a baby shower. Appropriate gifts can be found in the baby departments of most larger department stores. Blue is the traditional color for boys, while pink is the color for girls. Some contemporary American mothers-to-be prefer not to receive such traditional colors. Neutral, but acceptable colors are yellow and violet. Again, gifts can be as practical as diapers or as impractical as a lace bib. Stuffed animals are always good baby gifts.

Finally, we come to the subject of funerals. A bouquet with a small card may be sent before the funeral if you were close to the person who died or if you know one of his family members quite well. You might even share the cost of the bouquet with another friend or a group of friends. Sometimes the family will suggest donations to a particular charity or cause as an appropriate memorial for the one who has died.

Besides learning more about how to buy gifts by reading etiquette books, asking your American friends is always a good idea. When you want to give a gift to an American, consider the following questions. What is the occasion? To whom are you planning to give the gift? What are that person's tastes? What is the best and most appropriate gift, all things considered? Something else important is always to make sure that the price tags and stickers are taken off before wrapping the gift!

Are you ready now to present an American friend with a gift? What if he or she gives you one first? Open it, show that you like it, and say thanks for this show of thoughtfulness. Later that day or the next write a brief thank-you note saying it again. Americans don't usually expect a return gift; just your thoughtful thank-you will be enough.

CHAPTER 5
UNDERSTANDING AMERICANS

5. Introduction

Human beings are products of their own cultural backgrounds. All of us are. The Americans are no exception.

In the process of learning about a culture different from our own, each of us should be cautious when making value judgments, for they are almost always based on a set of cultural values and beliefs that we tend to take for granted. As a result, we rarely give much conscious thought to our own assumptions and behaviors. We assume that what we do and believe is "natural" and appropriate, and that any behavior that differs substantially from ours is not only "unnatural," strange, and unpredictable, but is inappropriate. Even when we think we are being objective in our judgments, we usually are not. These subjective judgments distort reality and, therefore, retard the growth of intercultural understanding and empathy.

How can we avoid such kinds of assumptions and judgments? What can we do to enhance the growth of authentic cultural understanding and empathy? John W. Gardner, a well-known American statesman and author, was once quoted as having said:

> *"You will never advance far in your understanding of another culture if you devote yourself to exclaiming that some things about it are wonderful and other things are terrible. This comes under the heading of entertainment and should not be confused with understanding. No society is all good or all bad, and the discovery that any particular society is compounded of both good and bad is not a very impressive finding. What you must try to do is to understand what problems a society faces; why it has developed the way it has; why it has certain characteristics rather than others; why it does some things so well and other things very badly."*

This chapter hopes to contribute toward that end. It continues what was begun in the previous chapter by taking us beneath the American facade to a level that allows us to view Americans within the context of their own cultural background. As a result, they should help diminish easy stereotypical judgments about Americans and build empathy for them.

The first two articles will offer us a view of some important American cultural patterns and values, as seen through Chinese and Peruvian eyes, while the third article will explore, from a Japanese perspective, the ways in which Americans learn their cultural patterns and values at home and at school. Then two young women, one Indonesian and the other Japanese, will share their perspectives on the role of contemporary American women, as well as their view of the role of modern women around the world. Finally, a Vietnamese immigrant and a Japanese housewife reveal to us their observations on the treatment of the elderly in American society.

UNDERSTANDING AMERICAN CULTURAL PATTERNS AND VALUES

Ai Lien Chiang
Taiwan

Many foreign students have come to the United States for a better education and an opportunity to meet Americans who are friendly, considerate, generous, and warm-hearted. Because of the differences in culture, customs, and life experiences, these wonderful fantasies about Americans soon disappear. Unfortunately, most foreign students come to believe that most Americans are "too selfish, too superficial, too free, too wasteful, too . . ., too . . ., too . . ." Many students end up feeling a great deal of bitterness.

I have gone through the same experiences. But after two and a half years of living in the United States, if anyone were to ask me what I thought of Americans, I could honestly say, "I like them." You see, my attitudes toward Americans are a lot better than they used to be.

How could I have changed my views? I certainly didn't change the ideas and values that are really important to me. I did, however, make a lot of adjustments and compromises in areas which I found were not as important to me as I once thought. One thing I have learned, relearned, and am still learning is this: the reason a person behaves the way he does is due a great deal to his cultural background. That includes not only them and me, but you, too. Therefore, one of the best ways to understand Americans and get along with them is to understand their cultural values and background. Some of the values important to understanding Americans are: the American emphasis on the importance of the individual; the peculiarly American concept of friendship; the striving for equality for all people, regardless of their social status, sex, race, religion, or age; and the emphasis on progress and change.

The most important and most basic characteristic of American culture is individualism. Daniel Boorstin, the well-known sociohistorian, has written that " . . . of all American myths, none is stronger than that of the loner moving west, across the land.... [This] pioneering spirit is a synonym for individualism." The pioneering spirit, handed down to the present generation of Americans from their American forefathers, includes the concepts of self-reliance, self-actualization, autonomy, and personal growth. So, the seeming self-centeredness of the American child, for example, is seldom questioned by parents or teachers. It is implicitly accepted that each person, whether he be an adult or a child, should be encouraged to make his own decisions, develop his own opinions, solve his own problems, and have his own possessions. In general, Americans learn to view the world from their own point of view, that of the individual self.

A second aspect of American culture shared by most Americans is the concept of friendship. Given the American values of self-reliance and self-actualization, we can realize why Americans tend not to have long and deep friendships. Though their personal relationships seem to be marked by friendliness, Americans tend to avoid personal commitments that might bring obligations. They simply do not like to get involved. If an American smiles at you, that smile may not mean what a smile means in your country. It may mean no more than an acknowledgement of your presence. In the same way, if you meet an American, he might say, "I'll call you," but he never does, or he might suggest, "Let's get together," and the two of you never do.

Another example of friendly, but impersonal, behavior may occur in work relationships with Americans. During working hours, they may be joking and talking with you and making you feel included. Then, as soon as working hours are over, their behavior seems to change. They act as if they hardly know you any more and don't even include you in any of their personal activities. Many of us from foreign countries have "comprehensive" or "whole" friendships that include all aspects of our lives. Americans usually do not. American friendships tend to be compartmentalized; certain friendships revolve around work or school activities while others revolve around church or club activities. Some even revolve around the family. Friendships that are centered around the office often do not spill out into recreational or even school activities.

A third aspect of American culture is the emphasis placed on equality. Edward Stewart, a well-known expert on American culture, noted that in most American social relationships, "each person is ascribed an irreducible value because of his humanness. When a personal confrontation is required between two persons of different hierarchical levels, there is an implicit tendency to establish an atmosphere of equality." For instance, many American children talk to their parents just as they talk to their friends. Sometimes you can see a man treating a woman as if she were another man. You will also encounter females working in occupations that are usually filled only by men in your country, such as truck driving, mail delivery, and coal mining. The employer is not supposed to show any discrimination against females or males. Outwardly at least, most differences between people, such as age, sex, race, religion, and class differences are diminished. There is an acknowledged emphasis on equality for all.

A fourth important aspect of American culture is the value placed on progress. In three different areas, we can see how the value of progress affects the American people. The first concerns the relationship between parents and their children. Most foreign students have been raised to respect their parents. They consider and value highly what their parents have taught them. Moreover, what their parents have taught them has generally become their own standard for living. Because of the idea of progress, most American children believe that their parents' ideas and standards are not necessarily the best. Americans think that there is always some change to be made for the better. A second area affected by the idea of progress concerns the material world. Many Americans assume that there are enough material goods for everyone; they tend to think that the supply is endless. So they are always trying to work for more, more, and still more. A third area involves the American's concept of time. They are very time-conscious, perhaps because time is such an important factor in the world of business and material acquisition. Americans tend to live by the motto, "Time is money." They believe you should use your time well and get the most that you can from it.

Being aware of the American emphasis placed on individualism, equality and progress, as well as understanding the way in which American friendships operate, can help the foreign student in his or her adjustment to American life and in the formation of more fulfilling relationships with American people. If you acknowledge and understand these American values, you will realize that Americans look at everything from their own cultural points of view, just as you do. If you consider their behavior from this vantage point, you might not say that Americans are *too* selfish or *too* superficial. Try to be aware of this when you meet and get to know Americans, and you will eventually find Americans with whom you might like to form friendships. You'll have to take a few chances and work at forming a friendship with someone whom you can trust, confide in, and share happy moments with. Maybe they might be only a tennis partner or a classmate or someone you work with. Having one friend is better than having no friend; having two friends is better than having one friend. It's up to you.

Since we know that friendships among Americans originate around activities, join more activities in order to meet more people. Go to a school activity or a church meeting; join a club on campus or participate in school athletics. The concept of equality in American society has positive sides too. There is always an equal opportunity for everyone. You'll have many opportunities to develop your career, talents, and a few good friendships.

What we can conclude from our discussion of American cultural values is that the more we know, the more we understand; the more we understand, the less we judge; the less we judge, the more we are open to people; the more we are open to people, the easier it will be to develop good relationships with them. And finally, the better our relationships with Americans are, the more we will enjoy our American experience.

Note: I want to give special thanks to Mr. Edward C. Stewart, the author of *American Cultural Patterns,* who provided me with a framework from which to view American culture and values.

VIEWING AMERICAN BEHAVIOR THROUGH FOREIGN EYES

Rosa Flores de Avila
Peru

No essay has seemed to me as difficult as writing about American traits and behavior, both good and bad. How can I judge correctly if I have lived here in the United States for only a few years? Besides, I can hardly judge even my own ethnic group. Perhaps it's not difficult to point out the characteristics of a culture; what is difficult is to label them good or bad and be fair about it. Who could do it? Sometimes while thinking about some characteristics, my mind said, "This is a good one," by my heart replied, "No, this is a bad one."

So, in this essay about culture, at moments the heart prevails, at others the mind. I will begin by enumerating the bad traits so that I can finish with this unpleasant task.

Something which I cannot get used to in the United States is seeing the situation in which older people live. I have seen aged people who during Christmas time had as sole company their TV sets. If living in such solitude during the whole year is bad enough, how would it be at Christmas?

In the United States, children have the right to denounce their parents to the authorities if they think they are abused. Once I was eyewitness to an incident. A little child who had lived in the country long enough to know this rule told his Latin mother, when she urged him to go to school, "If you continue bugging me, I will turn you in to the police." The woman gave her son a tremendous slap in the face as she said, "This is for you, and there will be a better one for the policeman who dares to come." Later, I saw them walking up the street laughing and holding each other's hands. This American rule is one I do not understand.

Each culture has a different way of appreciating its country's patriotic symbols. One day to my surprise, I saw how a teacher, for want of a pointer, took the American flag, wrapped the cloth of the flag around its pole, and made it the most original pointer that I had ever seen. After that experience, I noted without surprise how the design of the American flag is reproduced on suitcases, jackets, and even on a tiny bikini that a smiling mannequin was wearing on the cover of *Playboy Magazine*.

There is another custom that is very original too. Sometimes I have been asked, "May I ask you a personal question?" How could anyone say no, especially if one doesn't know what the question is going to be? Then after this innocent introduction comes a question that I would not dare to ask even my own sister.

Americans have the mania of shortening their words. Mathematics for Americans is math. Hippopotamus is hippo; in my opinion, an animal of that size must be called h-i-p-p-o-p-o-t-a-m-u-s. In the same way, even great personalities are not free from the application of this fad. Hence, it would not be strange for one to read: "Hey, come on in and admire King Tut's treasures." Tutankhamen, yes, is the name of a king, but Tut! To me, Tut sounds as if it were the name of a pet.

Americans are very direct people. They usually say clearly what they want. The first invitation that I ever received in this country said, "Bring your own bottle" or simply "BYOB." I have to confess that I was tempted not to attend the dinner. On another occasion, the hostess said to a group of people whom she was inviting, "Bring your own bottle and cigarettes; those who want to smoke can do it out of the house because I don't like my house smelling of tobacco." I wanted to suggest using a local park as the site for the party; besides, I was confused because if we brought our own supplies, why should I have to call her a hostess?

Some American traits have impressed me favorably. Americans generally feel quite proud of themselves when they have attained fortune and prestige through their own effort. While a Latin person would hide his past poverty, an American would mention his past at every opportunity.

To be energetic is considered a virtue in the United States. This can be appreciated easily in any activity that they pursue. Modern-style dance is an example. An American can contemplate Shirley MacLaine's dancing, feel enthusiastic, and even more, identify with the vigor that she shows. I personally, and possibly most all of my countrymen, would feel exhausted watching her.

It is a pleasure to attend a party in the United States. One is not obligated to eat if one doesn't want to. The hostess doesn't feel upset if one passes indifferently in front of the buffet table. It is completely different in my culture; the hostess would take it as a personal affront if one didn't eat the food and even if one didn't have a second helping of the abundant and varied dishes that she had made herself.

The American seems to eat very little, or at least Latin people think in this way; hence, I was advised to "eat before you go to an American party." I assure you that I never do that; I simply eat at home after the party.

The theme of this essay has been American behavior, but any person who reads this will learn very little about Americans; instead, he will learn a lot about Latin American people, or at least this Latin American person, since when a person writes about people of a different culture, what he usually does is to portray himself. For example, an Italian will say, "The American eats little," but a Japanese will say, "The American eats too much"; an Englishman or a Swede will say, "The American is too expressive and too demonstrative," while the Latin American will say, "The American is too cold." So the saying, "Nothing is either true or false; it is the thinking, that makes it so," can be used perfectly in this situation.

BRINGING YOURSELF UP AMERICAN
(Sorry, You Are Too Late!)

Misato Muchizuki
Japan

Have you ever felt that Americans are different from the people in your country? Do Americans exhibit characteristics different from the ones you are used to? You must have heard that Americans are characteristically independent and individualistic, some even say selfish and egocentric.

The first two words, *independent* and *individualistic,* describe the American personality accurately, while *selfish* and *egocentric* are judgmental and show little cultural understanding. I have studied in an American college for some time now. I used to think of Americans as selfish and egocentric, but now I recognize the cultural base of independence and individualism in their behavior and attitudes.

If we take a look at American history, we will quickly realize why it was necessary for people to become so independent and individualistic. Old habits and patterns die hard. Although independence and individualism have been a positive force in the establishment of the American nation, they have also been negative and counterproductive. American interpersonal and international relationships have been adversely affected by self-interest, individualism, and independence in an increasingly *inter*dependent world.

In school, Americans tend to be quite independent. Their teachers often encourage them to be so. In class after class, American students ask lots of questions while Asian students remain quiet and politely passive. Sometimes questions asked by American students seem pointless, sometimes merely rhetorical. The American students often seem to be demonstrating their independence of thought.

Americans would probably never understand or accept the philosophy of Japanese schools: What the teacher says is what the students remember. This is a common Japanese idea of what getting an education is all about. It seems that the philosophy of American schools is that what the student says is what the students remember. As would be expected, Japanese students ask far fewer questions than American students. This demonstrates a basic difference between the active American style education and the passive Japanese style, between a student-oriented educational system and a teacher-oriented one.

The American system is designed to encourage students, no matter how independent and individualistic they are to start with, to become more so. Foreign students often have problems with this type of school system because they aren't used to it. Foreign students often feel that there is too much freedom of choice and too many choices and, therefore, they feel they need guidance. They often expect their teachers and the school counselors to offer this kind of help. They also expect their teachers to push and pull them through their course work while their American teachers expect them to push and pull *themselves* through.

Foreign students often prefer tough, more structured classes to the lax, more informal ones that American students prefer. Even foreign students who long for freedom expect someone to help or push them to study in the same way that their teachers did in their own countries. Foreign students often voice a common complaint: "American teachers are not strict enough." They generally feel that if their teachers were more strict and demanding, they would study more. Even American students might agree but wouldn't like it if they couldn't speak their own minds, openly and directly ask questions, and confront their teachers when they didn't agree with them.

At what age do Americans start to learn to become so independent and outspoken? In grade school? In high school? In college? Actually, Americans begin to learn independence soon after they are born; some psychologists say it even begins before birth while the baby is still in the womb! What is certain, however, is that at a very young age, American babies and toddlers become more independent and aggressive than Japanese babies, who are generally more dependent and passive.

In many Asian countries, children are kept close to their mothers for longer periods of time than American children. Some Japanese babies even sleep with their mothers up until the age of three or four. American babies might sleep in a crib in the same room as their parents, but after several months the child is usually moved into his own bedroom. Then, too, while most Japanese women pick up their babies the moment they begin to cry, most American mothers will not pamper their babies in quite this same way. They expect their babies to do a certain amount of crying and do not worry so much about it unless the baby's crying persists. Japanese children rely on their mothers far more than American children do and aren't encouraged to express themselves in the direct and independent way that American children are.

This kind of behavior is fostered later on in the school systems. Japanese children are encouraged to consider the group above their own individual needs, and to look for the same sheltering and sense of belonging in their school as they had at home and as they will later find in most groups and workplaces in Japanese society. Quite the opposite occurs in American schools, where children are expected to work independently and to compete with other students for top grades and honors.

If you leave your country at an early age, that is before the age of five, you will get used to the American emphasis on independence and self-reliance, as well as the importance placed on self-expression and self-fulfillment. Even if your parents keep their own customs, you will be greatly influenced by the American educational system and the behavior all around you in American society. This may cause problems at home, where your parents and family members will be expecting you to keep the customs of your native country. Even if you came to the United States between the ages of six and ten, you will probably have a better chance of adjusting to both cultures. You will learn the difference between the two cultures, and you will still be flexible enough to move easily in both. If you have come to the United States at a much older age, you will have lost a lot of that flexibility. At some point you will never be able to recapture the time when children learn to become American and yet retain old cultural values and behaviors.

As we have seen, children learn their values and attitudes from their parents, the schools that they attend, and the society at large. It affects everything people do; this is true of the Japanese, the Americans, and all other peoples of the world. At some point, you are no longer young enough to grow up as a member of another culture. Therefore, it is too late for most of us to be brought up or to bring *ourselves* up American. The United States is the land of independence, self-sufficiency, and individualism; this is the country where people are ashamed to depend on someone else or to admit that they might need to do so. Perhaps growing up in another place has instilled in us the idea that we are indeed interdependent . . . as individuals and as nations. Perhaps this is something which we can help the Americans to realize little by little.

UNDERSTANDING AMERICAN WOMEN

Linda Kodrat
Indonesia

Women around the world have common bonds that unite them. Most women experience having babies, taking care of families, managing homes, cooking meals, and nurturing others. In spite of these common bonds, women around the world also have cultural differences. Even though these differences are important, it's often difficult for foreign students to talk about them with Americans. As the language barrier disappears, foreigners begin to make American friends and gain insight into the feelings, attitudes, and aspirations of American women.

Most foreign women grow up in societies where marriage is their primary goal. It used to be that way, too, for American women. Now, however, a career has often replaced marriage and family as the most important goal. As a result, American women seem much more independent than women from other cultures. On the other hand, many foreign women still prefer being more dependent than independent, being cared for by a husband, and not having to work outside the home.

According to a recent college survey, most American women think of themselves as highly independent. The trend is for them to continue working after marriage. Because of the high rate of divorce in the United States, many are single parents. These women have the double burden of working and bringing up their children. Many use baby-sitters when their children are very small, but when the children are a little older, mothers often have difficulty finding after-school care. Their children learn to become independent at an early age and sometimes get into trouble because of the lack of parental guidance and support.

Some American women feel that they are able to do any job that a man does, or at least they say that they are. For a number of years, many American women's organizations have tried to get the American Congress to pass the famous Equal Rights Amendment, which says women should enjoy full equality to men. So far, the Equal Rights Amendment has not become law because not enough states have ratified it yet. Still, the women's groups continue to work toward that end.

Because American women are quite independent, they often appear stronger and more aggressive than women in Asian or Latin cultures. Many of them "wear pants," both figuratively and literally, although on occasion they too like to dress up, act in feminine ways, and be "treated like ladies." Some of the qualities that they look for in their future husbands are empathy, sensitivity, intelligence, kindness, honesty, and loyalty. Aren't these also the qualities that we foreign women often look for in our future husbands?

One of the advantages that American women have over their foreign sisters is a lot more freedom to pursue their own ambitions without having to ask permission of anyone, including parents and family. If you understand all these facts about American women, you will feel less intimidated by them and will find it easier to make friends with them. Perhaps you will even gain a little of that confidence and independence for yourself.

ARTICLE
5.5

WOMEN, WHAT'S YOUR PLACE?

Ikuyo Andoh
Japan

Contemporary women are "caught between the devil and the deep blue sea" when they must decide whether to have a family, a career, or a combination of both. Many of us from other countries share this dilemma with American women, who have been struggling with the question for a long time. Some of these women are trail blazers who have faced matters squarely and made difficult choices. The road has not been easy for them, nor does it appear to be getting any easier for most contemporary women. There are, however, success stories in the United States.

Many American women are now working in various fields, either full-time or part-time. Some well-educated women have entered such male-dominated professions as business, law, and medicine. They have struggled against great obstacles and have often paid a high price emotionally in order to make inroads to the so-called "man's world." They have generally earned less than men of the same age and experience in similar job situations. Although women's job options still remain somewhat limited, opportunities are gradually increasing.

Some people ask why women work, especially those women who work even though they are married and would normally stay home. Some American women have to work to support their families, for many are now the sole breadwinners of their families, while others are supplementing their husbands' salaries. Still others work in pursuit of a career, just as men do, or in pursuit of knowledge and excitement to escape the boredom of home. Some women take great pride in their careers just as traditional women take pride in their families. And some women take pride in both.

What choice makes for the happiest woman? Women who espouse women's liberation say that a successful career brings women happiness and fulfillment; on the other hand, women who oppose women's liberation say that being a traditional wife and mother does. So who is right? And are American women happy? In the United States today, "happy" traditional women as well as "happy" career women seek counseling or psychological therapy. Therefore, there is a crack in the happy facade, for women who don't work often feel unfulfilled and have low self-esteem, and career women often feel unfulfilled in their personal lives.

Those who decide to do both must balance their home lives and work lives with a minimum of frustration. How do they do this? One way is to hire housekeepers or baby sitters; another is to ask their husbands to give up more of their time to help at home. However, men often aren't willing or used to doing this. Some men doubt their masculinity and positions in society if they do "women's work" at home. What about day-care help? Although it can help alleviate some of the burden of child care, some women feel guilty when their children are raised in day-care centers or by baby-sitters.

Women must continue to struggle with these issues for which there are no easy answers. How we all handle this basic conflict will affect not only our lives, but the lives of future women as well. Since women need role models, and most women aren't lucky enough to have good ones outside the traditional role models, we must often be our own role models. Perhaps some of us will also become the role models for our daughters and granddaughters, and thereby make the road a little easier for them than it has been for us.

Thanks to American women, however, it is now easier to answer the question: "Women, what's your place?" As a well-known saying reminds us: "A woman's place is in the home." I agree! A woman's place is in the home . . . and in business, in medicine, in education, and wherever else her career or interests lead her.

UNDERSTANDING THE OLDER CITIZEN OF AMERICA

Ngoc-Yen Ha
Viet Nam

Do you ever think about old people in American society? Most younger people are not interested in this subject. However, they should care about it now because eventually they will reach old age, too.

In America old age normally begins sometime after reaching the age of 65. At this age, people begin to retire from their jobs, become less active in their communities, and start to receive their Social Security benefits. They are now ready to begin their "second life" with free time and hobbies, travel and friends, gardens and grandchildren. On the other hand, some older people as they become less and less involved with people and community life, begin to live a more colorless existence and end up feeling lonely and miserable. Each person's circumstances and options differ. How much money is at his disposal? Do his grown children live nearby? Has he maintained the friendships that he formed while he was younger? Does he still enjoy good health? Answers to these questions vary from person to person and will make the difference between a happy old age and an unhappy one.

Changes In Old Age

Many physical, mental, and emotional changes take place in people as they get older. Some of these changes are positive; others are not. On the negative side, older people gradually begin to lose their ability to see and hear well. Some people become quite forgetful; others become physically ill or lose their desire to participate fully in life's many activities. Sometimes they even undergo behavioral changes, such as beginning to act again in very childlike or childish ways. As Shakespeare himself wrote once: " . . . an old man is twice a child."

In reality, old age is a time when people should be experiencing kindness and affection similar to what their parents gave them when they were children. Many older people in the United States experience just the opposite . . . loneliness and isolation . . . and no one who cares.

Where Old People Live

Most older Americans who are still healthy maintain their own independent style of life. Some continue to live where they have always lived; others sell their homes and buy or rent town houses or condominiums; and still others decide to live in retirement communities where they can enjoy the companionship of other older people and the convenience of recreational and social activities. A few even decide to live with their families, while the less fortunate are forced, because of illness or inability to care for themselves, to live in nursing or old people's homes. Nursing homes, even the most expensive and exclusive ones, are usually sad places to visit. Perhaps the saddest time to visit is during the holidays when the staff is often concerned more about their own family reunions than about the older people whom they take care of. In the worst homes, conditions are unpleasant: food is tasteless and poorly prepared, sheets and blankets are old and full of holes, and there are always odors that sicken the visitor. Yet one old man in a nursing home told me, "Well, at least I have a place to stay; I have to be grateful for that."

Do Americans Treat Their Parents Fairly?

Most foreigners, especially people from Asia and Latin America, believe that Americans do not treat their parents fairly. They think of the older people whom they knew at home; most of them were cared for well by their sons and daughters. Most adult children at home wouldn't think of sending their parents to a nursing home to live among strangers.

Many people from foreign countries have only known life as part of an extended family and don't understand the operation of the typical American-style nuclear family which consists of a father, mother, and children. Maids and other servants are rarely found in the United States. Therefore, all of the burden of household chores falls on the immediate family members.

Foreigners would be less critical about how Americans treat their elderly if they could experience life firsthand as an American. Self-sufficiency and independence from one's family are important personal goals in the United States. Most people in America are busy with their careers, their families, and their own lives. Nobody has enough time to take care of his own needs, let alone the needs of elderly people who require a lot of attention. The older people themselves prefer to live alone and to depend not on their families, but on themselves and their own Social Security and retirement funds. It is for these reasons, then, that people end up in nursing homes where they will be cared for on a daily basis and get the medical attention that they need.

Family members usually try to visit the elderly as often as they can. However, such visits are often depressing, and the younger people don't always feel comfortable. Maybe it reminds them of their own eventual old age and the possibility that they, too, will one day be confined to such a residence.

How The Aged Feel

No one wants to grow old in America. Most Americans view growing old as a negative experience, a time when people lose their usefulness and value as fully productive members of society. In Asian countries, people generally look forward to growing old because they will become the patriarchs and matriarchs of their societies, loved and respected by all. They expect to be well taken care of by their sons and daughters, who as children were well taken care of by them. Of course, this is the ideal and, even in Asian countries, it isn't always so wonderful to grow old. Yet nowhere else in the world, perhaps, do people fear the loneliness and decrepitude of old age as much as the Americans do.

VIEWING THE AMERICAN ELDERLY THROUGH JAPANESE EYES

By Kumiko Urayama
Japan

A May day of blue skies and soft breezes is always likely to produce a bout of spring fever and a desire to be outside. So it was for me one Saturday a year ago, shortly after I arrived in Los Angeles from Japan.

On that day, my family and I decided to enjoy a picnic in a local park. As we strolled along in search of a place to picnic, we passed young lovers holding hands, babies in mothers' arms, laughing children running and playing, amateur musicians strumming guitars, young people singing and clapping their hands in time to the music, dogs wagging their tails, and wisps of smoke filled with the aroma of barbecued chicken and *shish kebab*.

Suddenly an old woman caught my eye. She was sitting by herself on a bench. Her dress was shapeless and drab, her stockings unkempt, and her shoes old and scuffed. For a moment, time stopped; her image held my attention. I walked closer, and this time I looked directly into her grey and wrinkled face. Her expressionless eyes stared blankly into space. I heard her muttering under her breath, but she was not talking to anyone except herself, not even to a tired-looking old man sitting next to her.

What a contrast! In the midst of such a bright and happy atmosphere, this old woman seemed detached and isolated. I wondered if she had any children to care for her or anyone to share a picnic with. Did she have a place to call home and something productive to do with her time? Or was she the stereotype of the "senior citizen" in America about whom I had heard so much?

Since then I have become increasingly concerned about the treatment of old people in America. I have asked Americans how they feel about growing old and whether they preferred to live alone or with their children. Their responses are almost always the same: they prefer to live independently without imposing on their children. Even after they are much older and no longer in good health, they continue to insist on not being a burden to their children. These answers surprised me, for they were very different from those the Japanese would have given.

In Japan, parents usually continue to live with one of their children, usually the eldest son after his marriage. Even though a growing number of Japanese parents live separately from their children, most older Japanese still live with their children, especially as they become older, disabled, sick, or after spouses die.

Why do most of the elderly in Japan prefer to live with their children while most of the elderly in America prefer to live independently? Social Security and private pension systems have made it possible for Americans to do so. More importantly, American society is based on the concepts of individualism and personal autonomy, while Japanese society is based on the concept of dependence on other members of a particular group.

Interwoven with these Japanese ideals is the concept of *amae* which underlies all Japanese relationships. According to Takeo Doi, a well-known Japanese psychiatrist who wrote a book about it called *The Anatomy of Dependence, amae* expresses a universal need among all human beings. In English the closest translation of *amae* is *indulgent love,* the kind of love that all normal infants feel toward their mothers. It basically refers to the need or desire to be loved passively.

The Japanese continue to value and foster *amae* relationships throughout their entire lives. *Amae* is like the oil of Japanese society; it keeps social relationships running smoothly. It operates in almost all relationships, including those of family, work, and school. Members of each group, the insiders *(uchi no),* depend on and help other group members whenever there is a need; outsiders *(soto no)* or those who don't belong to the same group, are therefore not considered in that way. Perhaps that is why the Japanese would not consider putting their parents in homes as Americans do.

The parent-child relationship, according to Doi, is the most deeply and naturally dependent and interdependent. In this relationship the greatest degree of *amae* is permitted. Therefore, it is natural for elderly Japanese parents to depend on their adult children in the same way that their children depended on them when they were younger.

Americans, on the other hand, reject this kind of dependence and try to live lives that are quite remote from the "world of *amae.*" American people learn from early childhood that independence and self-reliance are the most important characteristics of a happy and successful life. Therefore, it's natural for the American elderly not to depend on their children as they grow older.

I used to believe that elderly Americans must lead very sad and lonely lives, but, as I talked with a number of older Americans, I found that their lives seemed more exciting and vivid than the lives of many older Japanese . . . as long as they remained in good health and didn't suffer any financial problems. In Japan, satisfaction depends mainly on the relationship between parent and adult child. As long as they have happy relationships, they live comfortably. However, some Japanese live lives of mental isolation because their children subtly let them know that they are unwanted. Some older Japanese live more isolated lives than if they were physically living alone. If the American elderly feel this sort of loneliness, at least they are used to being alone.

Yet, I wonder if the American elderly living alone are still comfortable after they grow too old and feeble to care for themselves. Many of those I talked to said that nursing homes were miserable places and were also terribly expensive. According to a recent

Newsweek magazine article, the average nursing home cost is about $1,500 a month, or $18,000 a year. This kind of cost could quickly exhaust the savings of most elderly people. What a high price to pay for independence!

However, *Newsweek* also reported that an estimated 76 percent of the old lived independently, while 18 percent lived with an adult child. Relatively few lived in complete isolation; in fact, 80 percent saw a close relative at least once every week, and only 5 percent lived in nursing homes. Yet fear and uneasiness about the future increase the older they get.

The support systems for the elderly seem more highly developed in America than in Japan. Whatever support systems for the elderly are provided, however, they won't bring happiness or satisfaction to the elderly if emotional support is not also provided. In this particular area, we Japanese seem much more sensitive and considerate because we try to understand the feelings of others.

The other day I spoke to a very old woman in the supermarket who seemed to need some help. When I asked if I could help, she began to tell me the story of her life. Tears filled her eyes, and I felt that she must be a terribly lonely person. She had lived alone for more than sixty years, she told me, and had no children. Nevertheless, she insisted that she had never felt lonely and had never thought of depending on others; she had never known another way of living. I seemed to have penetrated her inner heart. Otherwise, why the tears in her eyes? This old woman, who lived in the world repressing her desire for *amae,* would have accepted *amae,* if she had been Japanese living in Japan. As Doi says in his book, all people have a deep and innate need or desire for *amae,* even those who grow up believing that they don't.

I basically agree with him, but I can't judge which country's elderly are more comfortable because each lives in a different culture. I can say this with confidence, however: both the Americans and Japanese should think seriously and deeply about the problems of their elderly. After all, nobody can avoid old age and the problems that go with it.

CHAPTER 6
EXPLORING ASPECTS OF
AMERICAN CULTURE

6. INTRODUCTION

Another approach to understanding Americans better which is fun and invites your direct participation is the exploration of various aspects of American culture. It has been said, even by Americans themselves, that the United States has no special culture of its own. However, as you look at its holidays, national symbols, favorite sports and pastimes, and its emphasis on such technological developments as the computer, you will begin to realize that there is a strongly developed and unique culture here.

Exploring these cultural aspects will increase your understanding of Americans still further; doing so will also add to your growing collection of common American references, references which underlie much of American thinking, communication, and shared activities.

It is interesting to observe, in any given presidential election year, the ways in which the candidates use these aspects of American culture to appeal to the voters. It is almost always the presidential candidate who is able to manipulate American patriotic symbols and references in the most powerful ways that wins the election. In a similar way, your growing ability to make references that Americans make and to understand their national symbols and holidays will help you gain acceptance among Americans and allow you to converse with and get to know them more effectively and enjoyably.

Of all the holidays, Thanksgiving is probably the most widely celebrated by people of every religious and ethnic affiliation across the country. Although many Americans attend religious services on that day, it is still much more family-oriented and patriotic than religious. For this reason, an article on Thanksgiving is included in this chapter, rather than one exploring other American holidays, such as New Year's Day (January 1), Valentine's Day (February 14), Independence Day (July 4), or Christmas (December 25).

Of the symbols that all Americans recognize as patriotic, the cowboy not only has historical and patriotic significance, but is the epitome of the classic American hero. Other American symbols, such as the American flag, referred to as the "stars and stripes"; the American bald eagle; the Statue of Liberty; apple pie; or motherhood might have been explored. Yet, none are quite as all-pervasive and deeply significant as the cowboy, symbol to Americans of a real heroic type.

In technology, the computer has revolutionized American life. Forms of transportation like the automobile, space exploration, "Star Wars" concepts, VCR's, and food processors have done so too. None have captured the imagination of Americans in such a variety of ages, occupations, and interests as has the computer, however, and none have affected so many aspects of American life.

Finally, concerning entertainment and sports, the ultimate American sport is football, not basketball, tennis, or even baseball, although these sports have strong followings, too. American football is perhaps the most popular sport in America, especially among men, and embodies important American values and ideals. An American businessman who admitted to not being fond of the sport commented once, "If you want to make a sale in this country, make sure that you can talk football first!"

And if you, too, would like to make successful contacts here with Americans, try learning to "talk American," which might begin with experiencing a little of a typical American Thanksgiving Day.

THANKSGIVING DAY IN AMERICA

Satoko Watanabe
Japan

People in every country have their own shared traditions and holidays. Celebrations of traditions and holidays take place for a variety of reasons. One reason is to get together with family and friends and to share the celebration of a common theme. Traditions and holidays are rooted in historical fact, but after a certain number of years have passed, people begin to forget what actually happened. Yet, they continue to follow these same old traditions and beliefs, often without understanding the reality or origin of the events. Americans are no exception.

It has been commonly said that the Americans have no culture, no traditions. This couldn't be farther from the truth. We can see from the celebration of Thanksgiving Day that Americans have a strong sense of heritage. As foreigners, the better we know American traditions, the better we will understand their ways of thinking and acting and the easier it will be for us to communicate with the Americans.

Thanksgiving Day occurs each year on the last Thursday in November. An excellent way to know more about Thanksgiving is to accept an invitation to an American home for a traditional Thanksgiving dinner. The following recounts a typical Thanksgiving Day experience with an American family.

I rang their doorbell at 3:30 and waited nervously until the door opened. Finally the door opened. "Happy Thanksgiving! Please come in," said my American host. As I walked in, the wonderful but strange aromas from the kitchen greeted me. My host introduced me to his family and friends in the living room, about 16 people in all.

"Everything is ready," said his wife as she showed us to the dining room. The men immediately quit watching the football game on TV and followed her. I was impressed by the elegant table setting and the impressive variety of foods filling the large dining table; my mouth began to water. The host began to carve a huge turkey on the largest platter of all. After "grace," a short prayer of thanks, we all took our seats and began to help ourselves to the food. Someone helped me fill my plate high with mashed potatoes, turkey, dressing, cranberry sauce, and other foods that were new to me. Following the dinner, we were served a dessert, something called pumpkin pie. By 5 o'clock, we had eaten our fill of delicious food. Then I initiated the following conversation.

"Does your family often come together like this?" I asked my hostess. I had heard that American family life was not very close.

"Well! The last time we got together was last Thanksgiving. You know, everyone is so busy with their jobs, it takes a special holiday like Thanksgiving to give us a good excuse for a reunion. As for turkey and this kind of food, we rarely have it except on

Thanksgiving Day," she replied.

"Why is turkey so special?" I asked.

"Because of a tradition started by the early immigrants to America called Pilgrims. They hunted wild turkeys for their food. So, we like to follow the tradition," she answered with a smile.

The tradition of Thanksgiving is based partially on historical fact and partially on myth. In the 1600's, the Pilgrims, a religious group who had been treated cruelly in England, found their way to what is now Plymouth, Massachusetts, near Cape Cod, north of New York City. They suffered a terrible first winter in this strange new land. Many of them died, and the survivors had to fight hard to survive by raising corn and vegetables, and hunting the wild deer and turkey, which the Indians showed them how to do. The next year, the Pilgrims had a more successful harvest. In order to thank the Indians and their God for saving their lives and helping them win their battle against the many great dangers in a new land, they invited some of the Indians to a feast of Thanksgiving. Actually, the first feast was not held in November but at an earlier date.

For Americans, this holiday is a very emotional and popular one. New Americans begin to share in this tradition of a family time soon after they arrive because children learn about it in school. Based both on historical fact and national mythology, it is one of those cultural traditions that binds people together, and in this case incorporates new Americans quickly into the fabric of American society and tradition.

THE COWBOY SYMBOL OF AMERICA

Ana Maria Echeverri L.
Colombia

The American cowboy! Certain images immediately come to mind: a solitary man on horseback against a backdrop of a majestic landscape with mountains, boulders, cactuses, and endless sky. A closer look at this man reveals a gun at each hip, dusty cowboy boots, skin wrinkled and leathered by the sun, jaw set and determined, and a confident glint to the eye, hidden beneath the shade of his hat.

It is a majestic pose frozen in every American's mind. Then suddenly, the man on horseback is off at a gallop in quest of adventure and new horizons, in pursuit of a bandit, or to save a beautiful woman. He is ready to conquer the land, a woman, an enemy . . . a tough guy with a big and gentle heart. He is a truly romantic figure, the essence of heroic character and aspirations.

Yet, how different this concept or image is from the one we Latin Americans have of the same figure: the *llanero* of Colombia and Venezuela, the *gaucho* of Argentina, and the *vaquero* of Mexico. All share the wrinkled skin and dusty boots; here the concept changes, however. Instead of the lone, romantic, self-sufficient individual, we Latin Americans immediately think of the loneliness of the land separating the cowboy from the rest of humanity. He works hard in the middle of a landscape which is endlessly austere and inhospitable. There is little adventure in his difficult life style. Is he happy? Yes, we Latins think so. Is he heroic? No, not in our opinion. We just see him as a common man with a physically demanding life style. Could he capture the imagination of our people or be elected to the presidency of one of our nations? No, both are highly unlikely. Yet, in the United States, John Wayne is still a heroic figure years after his death, while Ronald Reagan, the cowboy politician, has been elected President.

Each culture has its own beliefs, values, and folk heroes which have developed over the years and have been passed on from generation to generation. As a result, they have become an integral part of the subconscious mind of a people. Heroes are not seen as fabricated or created myths or legends; they are accepted as fact and are as natural as the physical environment. Their existence is seldom open to question. We Latin Americans celebrate the family, respect it, and value it. The family is the base of our society; we believe that without it the entire society would disintegrate. For us, there is often a discrepancy between the family as myth and the family as reality. In North American society there is a discrepancy between the cowboy as sacred myth and the cowboy as reality, between the cowboy of many dreams and the cowboy as a down-to-earth human being.

To know a real cowboy, let's go back to a time when the American man lived in a different world, in an inhospitable environment where he worked hard to survive. At that time the western part of America was all open spaces, ranches, and homesteads; cattle and horse raising were among the most important activities. The cowboy often worked for someone else on a ranch. He took part in roundups or rodeos which consisted of gathering and branding cattle. He exhibited such qualities as strength, bravery, and agility. Maybe the cowboy was tall and handsome, but not always. He had a definite personality and a particular way of behaving; he did not always care what other people thought because he believed that what he was doing was right. Furthermore, he was often a lonely man without family ties.

He did not attempt to create beauty; facts were more important to him, and, as a consequence, he admired a man's "character" above his brain. He was usually loyal to his friends and served society without becoming part of it completely. According to his code, he developed his own philosophy. He felt in control of his own destiny, and as a result, he was an individualist. This individualism is reflected in his independence of character, his life of action, and the pursuit of his own interests. He considered himself free to make up his own mind, and every day was a challenge for him.

Over the years, the cowboy became less important, but because his actions were recognized and revered by the rest of the American population, he became a mythological man; he was admired and imitated for what he did. Superstars like John Wayne were created to portray the cowboy in films, and the myth was perpetuated. Today, many members of American society have modeled their behavior after the cowboy image. Many Americans have become like him. In every American is at least a secret part that is all-American cowboy, individualistic, in pursuit of worthy goals, and idealistic.

THE COMPUTERIZED AMERICAN WORLD

Wai Git Hui
People's Republic of China

Have you noticed the automatic tellers in banks, the fancy cash registers in supermarkets and department stores, and the typewriter-like machines which register you for college? Did you know that these are only a few of the many computers affecting your daily life in the United States? Time has always been money for the Americans. Because of their speed and accuracy in doing time-consuming tasks, computers have become part of every aspect of American life.

We can save a lot of time and money by understanding and using computers properly. A computer is nothing more than a machine which takes information (input), processes it, and gives results (output). We can perform most tasks more economically with a computer than we can without one. The results are often equivalent or superior in quality. It's no wonder that the computer is so widely used now in many areas of American life: in education, government, business, and even the home. Computers will certainly greatly affect your own life in the United States.

In Education

Nowadays, more and more teachers and students are taking advantage of the computer. Instructors can use computers to grade tests, store student grades, and calculate grade point averages, while students can use computers to calculate mathematical problems, draw graphs, compose music, write essays, and double check their grade point averages.

In educational institutions, computers can be used in a number of ways. They can help create administrative systems, solve problems, and develop integrated learning systems. Using the computer in school administration includes such tasks as the scheduling of teachers as well as the formation of student class programs. Making financial projections and keeping the accounting records of a school are often complicated tasks. The computer stores all of the pertinent information, juggles the facts and figures to make charts and graphs, and gives print-outs of all updated material so that the school administrators can make the best decision in a short period of time. Your school is no exception.

A good example of the computer as a problem solving tool is the smaller hand-held computer, the calculator. We can do calculations much faster with a calculator than we can by hand. In some mathematics classes, you have to have a calculator in order to finish your tests on time. The calculator and computer relieve students of repetitive calculations for simple arithmetic problem solving as well as complicated and time-consuming calculations.

Now a word about integrated learning systems or computer-assisted instruction. This has become extremely important in American institutions of higher learning, as well as in high schools and grade schools around the country. There are a number of advantages to this. Course material can be prepared by the best teachers of any given subject for use by all students. Each student can, therefore, receive individual instruction and proceed at his own speed.

In addition, a computer can readily supply information to a remote terminal which has a keyboard on which to type in the questions and a screen to display the answers. By using a home computer connected with a computer at school, we can study at home on our own time. Finally, the computer is very patient. If there is anything that a student does not understand, he can ask the computer as many times as he wants, and the computer will always give him the right answer.

There are also some disadvantages to computerized instruction. It is very difficult for a programmer to write a program that can answer all the questions that a student might ask. Computer-assisted instruction may also isolate students from each other, and some students who need the personal encouragement of an instructor may find it difficult to study by themselves. All in all, however, the advantages far outweigh the disadvantages.

In Government

The computer has made its way into all levels of government . . . national, state, and local. Governments use the computer to create forms, keep records, and to write reports; they also use it to file, process, retrieve, update, and store information. As governments have had to provide more and more services, and as they have developed more complex internal structures, doing all of the necessary paper work by manual, clerical procedures has become exceedingly difficult, costly, and time-consuming. Computers also save on storage space.

In Business

The computer has also invaded the business world and has changed it forever. It is used in small businesses as well as the larger ones by people at all levels of the organization. Banks, supermarkets, real estate agencies, publishers, retailers, wholesalers, import-exporters, and law firms are only a few of the many businesses that depend on the computer for all kinds of functions: keeping accounts, billing clients, doing payrolls. Banks, for example, now use automatic tellers which allow their clients to deposit and withdraw money at any hour of the day or night, or to move money from one account to another.

Whatever you do, from banking to starting your own business, the computer is a necessary part of it all. Even the "junk mail" you receive at your home is a result of the computer at work in the business world. Someone has put your name and address into his computer.

At Home

If you buy a home computer, a printer, and a word processing program, you can type and print letters and reports just as you would on a typewriter. However, it is much more convenient. When you make a mistake, you simply have to touch a few keys to make the correction; you don't have to use correction paper. When you know that your letter or report is free of errors, you can print it on your printer. Another advantage of a home computer is that it allows you and your friends to play a number of electronic games right in your own home!

Since there are so many advantages to the computer, and since computers are here to stay, it might be a good idea to start learning more about them. There are several ways to do it. You can ask your friends who know computers. You can buy books to study. Or you can simply take a class. Most schools offer a variety of classes, for the beginner as well as for the more advanced and sophisticated user. Once you have a computer, you will form a working relationship with it, one that just may blossom into one of the most rewarding love affairs of your life!

CRAZY ABOUT FOOTBALL?

Angela Chang
Taiwan

Most American men and some American women are *crazy* about football. You may be thinking of soccer, but I am referring to football, American style. Helmets, shoulder pads, knee pads, shoes with wicked-looking spikes, and brute strength, teamwork, and a strange-looking object called a "football," not to mention lots of pretty girls called cheerleaders in short skirts and bright colors, men called officials in black and white stripes, and thousands of cheering and/or booing fans. This is only part of American football.

Before I came here, I had never heard much about American football. Since coming here, I see evidence of football everywhere. Children play it on their school playgrounds, college students play it on weekends, spectators watch it on T.V. in games, sports news, and in commercials, and we all read about it in the sports sections of newspapers.

If you are like me, football seems strange, mostly because it is not popular in our own countries. It is often difficult for us to understand how so many Americans can find it so exciting. We can only draw the conclusion that American football is deeply embedded in American culture and is the product of fundamental American cultural values and attitudes. Considering football in this way will increase our interest in learning more about the game. We may never "love it" or be "crazy" about it as the Americans are, but we will certainly begin to appreciate it more. Since we need to see it in its cultural and historical perspectives, let us begin with a little history.

The game of football was started on November 6, 1869, at an informal meeting of male students from Rutgers and Princeton Universities on a field in New Brunswick, New Jersey. These young men spent the afternoon chasing a ball around before a small group of casual spectators. Little did they know that they had played the first game of American football and had started the United States on the road to its football craze. In a little more than one hundred years, America's love affair with football has become a deep commitment, like a solid marriage with no chance of divorce.

For most of us who watch football for the first time, it looks dangerously rough. Imagine what it would feel like to collide with a player from the other team who weighs over two hundred pounds — or to have the football and be brought down (tackled) by five players who form a mountain of bodies on top of yours. In reality, the players, even though they are well protected by the gear they wear, are trained physically and mentally for the shoving and tackling on the field. Yet such physical involvement would be unacceptable to many newcomers who do not enjoy the so-called contact sports, for American football is probably the one sport with the most contact.

Why do Americans like football so much? If we knew in what way football is very American, then we might know something about why it is so popular here. Here are some American cultural values that we can find in football.

A sense of fair play is one of America's important cultural values. Everyone has an equal opportunity for success (winning a touchdown or making a play). Yet he must follow the rules of the game to do so. If he loses a point or his team loses a game, he should be a good sport. A show of good sportsmanship is almost more important than anything, even winning. He must, therefore, acknowledge when the other team has won the game through skill and strategy.

American culture also values self-reliance, self-actualization, and individualism. All are stressed in the game of football and are necessary for the players to have, in addition to a strong body. The ability to bear up under physical and mental pressure is desirable to most Americans but essential in a football game.

The "American Dream" supposes that everyone with determination and hard work can become successful. So it is with the game of football. Football players can achieve success as they push themselves to their ultimate physical and mental limits. They must believe that they will accomplish the goals they have set. Good players never give up, even when they fail game after game. Good players use their brains at all times to remember coaches' instructions, to follow signals, and to try at all times to outguess the opposition.

The fans are full of American energy, enthusiasm, and spontaneity. Many take their families and drive long distances to the stadium. They almost forget who and where they are when they become involved in a game. They yell and wave flags to cheer their team on. When their team wins, they are as happy as if they themselves had won the game. If their team loses, they are disappointed but look forward to the next game with renewed confidence and enthusiasm.

As foreign students in the United States, how should we watch football? In order to enjoy it more fully, here are three suggestions that may help. While watching a football game, ask someone what is taking place and why. Second, do not just watch the ball. Remember that football is a team sport. The eleven players on each team play the game according to a set of rules involving the movement of the ball itself. The object is to run with and pass the ball over the opponents' goal line. Whichever team does this earns a touchdown and scores points. Finally, learn the rules. Ask someone who knows, and most Americans know quite a lot. Here are some basic terms peculiar to football:

a. The **team** is any number of players on one side. No more than eleven players from each team may be on the field at one time. Players usually specialize in either offense or defense; this is why, when a side changes from offense to defense or vice versa, all eleven players leave the field to be replaced by another eleven from the same side. Players further specialize in passing the ball, receiving passes, running with the ball, blocking, tackling, or kicking the ball. Sometimes a player specializes in more than one function. For example, a player on offense who does not receive a pass or run with the ball blocks for the teammate who does.

b. The **offense** is the team that has the ball and is trying to advance it toward the opponents' goal line. (Pronounced "OF-fense.")

c. The **defense** is the team that does not have the ball and is trying to prevent the other team from advancing toward its goal line. (Pronounced "DE-fense.")

d. **Quarters** are the four periods of playing time in a game, fifteen minutes each. If a game ends in a tie, an overtime may be played until one team makes a touchdown or a field goal and wins. In that case, the first team to score wins.

e. When a side has control of the ball, it is allowed four **downs,** or attempts to advance the ball ten yards towards the opponents' goal line. If successful, that side is allowed another four downs until it either fails to advance the ball ten more yards or makes a touchdown or a field goal.

f. A **touchdown** occurs when a player has crossed the goal line with the ball or has caught a pass there; it earns his team six points.

g. **Tackling** is causing an opponent with the ball to fall to the ground. At this point the play stops.

h. **Blocking** on offense is preventing, through physical contact, an opponent from tackling a teammate with the ball. On defense it is stopping a pass or a kick with a part of one's body.

i. A **pass** is a ball thrown forward from one team member to another.

j. An **interception** is catching an opponent's pass, thereby taking control of the ball away from the opponents.

k. A **bomb** is a long pass.

l. A **rush** occurs when team members run quickly with the football or move quickly to block a pass or a kick.

m. **Goal lines** are the lines at each end of the field used in determining a goal.

n. A **try** for an extra point is an attempt to kick the ball between the goal posts immediately after a touchdown. If successful, it is worth one point. A try done by running or passing the ball is worth two points.

o. A **field goal** is done by kicking the ball through the goal posts at any time other than immediately after a touchdown and is worth three points.

p. If by the fourth down a side obviously will not be able to advance the ball ten yards, it usually **punts** or kicks the ball far into the opponents' territory, thereby giving them control of the ball in a less advantageous position.

q. A side pays a **penalty** in the form of either a loss of yards or a loss of a down when it violates the rules. Penalties are often due to unnecessarily violent and dangerous actions, although many foreign observers may think that most of the actions are unnecessarily violent and dangerous.

Are you now a little more interested in football? Imagine: I am a woman, and I am almost becoming as "crazy" about football as some of those Americans mentioned earlier. But would American football become popular in Taiwan, Japan, or India? I have my doubts, mainly because of the differences in cultural values, yet only time will tell.

Note: I would like to express my appreciation to Alvar K. Kauti, Dean of Student Activities and former football coach at Pasadena City College, whose generosity in sharing his enthusiasm for and knowledge of football has made this article possible.

I would also like to thank George A. Hayden, Associate Professor of East Asian Languages at the University of Southern California, whose special hobby is games of strategy. His suggestions for definitions have helped me to present the fundamental terms of football in a more complete and understandable form.

CHAPTER 7
GETTING ADJUSTED

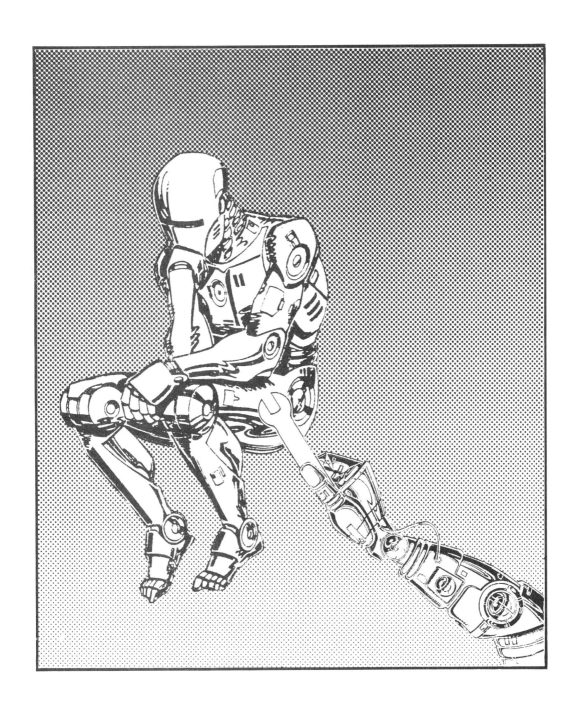

7. INTRODUCTION

*"I do not want my house to be walled in on all sides and my windows
to be stuffed. I want the cultures of all lands to be blown about my
house as freely as possible. But I refuse to be blown off my feet by any."*
Mahatma Gandhi

*Now that you are more familiar with your surroundings and with
American people, you may still be getting adjusted to life here so that you
feel less foreign. However, it is natural that old ways of approaching life
will still be very much a part of you and that you will have some difficulties
in accepting the American approach to life. Homesickness and nostalgic
longings are all part of the adjustment period in any foreign environment,
especially when it differs from your own. One difficulty may be your
struggle with the English language but another may come from cultural
differences, even just the routines of everyday life. In particular, you may
feel even more at odds if you are here to stay, knowing that, for whatever
reason, you may never be able to see your homeland again. This is
especially true for refugees from war-torn countries.*

*If your family is here, there may be conflicts in cultural values between
those of the parents, who often continue to live by the traditional values of
the homeland, and those of the children, who have to choose between the
values of home and the new values that they are learning at school and
among their American peers. For the children, in particular, there will be a
struggle for identity which will be more traumatic than for most American
children.*

*The traditional male-female relationships that were acceptable and
comfortable in your homeland may be in conflict with those less traditional
relationships here. Husband-wife and parent-daughter relationships can
undergo painful pressures, and those involved will be struggling to find a
new sense of equilibrium.*

*In spite of the difficulties, the moments of loneliness and struggle, there
will be a gradual adjustment for most of you which will make you stronger,
more confident adults. The stormy clouds will dissipate to be replaced by
the growing sense of accomplishment and peace. The following articles on
these topics have been written by individuals who have already gone
through the adjustment period. They have survived and been enriched by
their adjustment to a new and foreign environment.*

ADAPTING TO YOUR NEW LIFE IN THE UNITED STATES

Edward (Te-Lung) Chang
Taiwan

Cultural conflict is a term which will not be found in your dictionary. Yet it's one of the most important terms to be understood and faced by every foreigner who wants to have a successful stay in the United States. People of different cultural backgrounds often bring different languages, customs, and beliefs to a new place. When these people live together, cultural conflict is bound to take place. Naturally, foreigners will have some difficulty in adapting to their new environment.

When I first arrived in this country, cultural conflict was a big problem for me. How should I communicate with Americans? What were the most important customs here? How would I adjust my own life in order to adapt to this new society? This series of problems bombarded me and resulted in my getting homesick and withdrawing from my new environment.

However, I did try to talk with some other foreign students. I listened to their experiences, opinions, and ideas. As a result, I tried to eliminate from my life those factors which kept me from adapting to my new life in America. Although "cultural conflict" was not to be found in my dictionary, I was creating my own dictionary of invaluable concepts and terms.

Where are the differences that hinder us in adapting to a new culture? All foreigners experience them: a new language, new customs, new foods, and new religious beliefs.

Language

The first problem suffered by foreigners arriving here is the language. Not understanding English causes you to say all kinds of things which you don't mean. A friend asked for some fried rice with his dinner once. He found out later that the waitress understood him to say "flied lice." Another time, he was talking with an American friend about the national elections, but talked about the national "erections" instead. Of course, it embarrassed his friend, a girl.

Not understanding English will also cause you to misunderstand friendliness as pushiness, kidding as sarcasm, and a simple "thank you" as a lack of appreciation. Idiomatic expressions will confuse you: "Don't be such a turkey" may mean "Don't be a wet blanket."

Customs

Customs include many and diverse aspects of life in a country, even something as apparently insignificant as a wink. In my case, the American wink bothered me for almost six months. I could not understand its purpose, nor could I predict when it would occur. The first person to wink at me was a female cashier at my college; the next one was a female classmate; but when the next one came from a male instructor, I was thoroughly confused. What did it all mean? Were they simply being friendly? Or were they making fun of me? Or was it supposed to tell me something they didn't want to tell me verbally? I finally asked one of my American professors. She told me she had not noticed that anyone ever winked that much, and then she too winked at me. I knew that I was beginning to adapt to American culture the other day when a friend of mine who had just arrived from Taiwan asked me why I had just winked at him.

Customs also include the significance of color and the formalities that people follow during the holidays. As to color, an American woman would never wear red at her wedding or white at a funeral (black's the color), whereas a Chinese might wear red at her wedding and would definitely wear white at a funeral.

Food

Hamburgers, French fries, hot dogs ("hot dogs?!"), cheese, desserts immediately following dinner, popcorn . . . these are some American foods which are strange to foreigners. You wonder if that's all Americans know how to eat. It's all very misleading.

Some Americans actually enjoy good home-style cooking. If you're interested in this style of cooking, you can pick up an inexpensive book. You can also hope for an invitation to someone's home.

Another aspect of the American diet is choice. You can eat almost any imaginable cuisine here. A number of Americans have now cut down on their fat and sugar intake and are following a healthy diet. These Americans might pass up the opportunity to have a soft drink and French fries. Americans are also cutting down on smoking and drinking alcoholic beverages.

Religious Beliefs

If you come from a different religious background, American religious beliefs could be a problem for you. However, Americans have a basically liberal attitude toward religion, except for some of the "born-again" religious groups that have become so popular here among certain segments of the population. As for those groups, if you're interested, you can catch some of their programs on television.

If you're interested in finding out about different religious groups, most churches, synagogues, and temples welcome visitors. Just check the religious section of your local Saturday newspaper. Attending different kinds of religious services here could be quite an adventure and make you more aware of the varied cultural and religious heritage of the United States.

Keep a journal of your observations. Whenever something puzzles you, angers you, or intrigues you, write it down. A well-kept journal will be interesting reading long after you've forgotten the cultural conflict and confusion that you experienced when you first arrived. After all, how do you think I remembered the strangeness of the American wink?

ANTICIPATING AND COPING WITH HOMESICKNESS

Shiva Panahshahi
Iran

Getting homesick? Who, me? When I first came to the United States, I did not imagine that I would have a difficult time dealing with homesickness. My family had tried to prepare me for coping with this kind of emotional upset, and I felt well-prepared and strong enough to overcome any obstacle that might arise.

For the first few months, the novelty and excitement of being in a new country helped me sail right through. After the honeymoon period was over, my eyes opened to the reality of my situation: I was homesick, absolutely and unavoidably homesick. Talking to other foreign students, I found that most of them had experienced the same emotions. Homesickness is something that all foreigners face and must deal with. Feelings of sadness, restlessness, boredom, loneliness, and general depression are a few of the symptoms of being homesick.

Not everybody reacts in the same way. Some people overeat, others lose their appetites altogether. Some people cannot sleep at night; others escape from reality by oversleeping. Some students even start to question their motivation and lose sight of their goals. They feel lost and friendless. The problem intensifies when they find themselves unable to focus on their studies and, as a result, begin to accumulate poor grades.

What can be done to effectively deal with this paralyzing mental disorder? There are a number of ways to cope with this problem. Fortunately, most of us survive and eventually learn to manage the shock of a new culture. The first thing to remember is that time and a positive attitude will take care of most problems, even this one.

You must also recognize that you may never be entirely free of homesickness. These feelings should gradually subside to the point that they will not be as overwhelming as they were in the beginning. Talking with someone who has had similar experiences can be most helpful. Every American college and university has counseling services which can help students deal with such psychological difficulties as homesickness.

It is also important to keep yourself busy with a variety of activities, such as participating in sports, listening to music, watching TV, dancing, and spending time with friends. In addition, it is a good idea to join some special interest clubs on your campus or in the community.

Here are two words of warning, however. First, as you meet people and make new friends, do not imagine that you can solve your problems by getting casually involved with a member of the opposite sex. This kind of involvement can compound your problems rather than solve them. Second, you must guard against being "carried away" by the attractiveness of a new culture simply because you are trying to run away from your feelings of homesickness. If you ignore or change your basic beliefs and try to imitate American ways completely, you may lose both your identity and integrity and become a foreigner even to yourself.

If you have tried all of the above ways to rid yourself of homesickness and nothing has worked, you might consider going back to your country. However, this should be your last resort. Fortunately, like most foreigners, you will survive this malady called homesickness. All you need is a little patience, perseverance, and a willingness to "take the bull by the horns."

An age-old secret of survival in this world has always been "adaptability." The sooner you can adapt and assimilate, the better the chance that you will have a successful and happy experience in the United States or wherever else you might go. Once you overcome your homesickness, you will become a stronger and more independent person, who copes with any difficulty life may bring your way.

According to the American author John Cheever, "Homesickness is . . . absolutely nothing. Fifty percent of the people in the world are homesick all the time. . . . You don't really long for another country. You long for something in yourself that you don't have, or haven't been able to find." As long as you're homesick in the United States or anywhere, you are still looking for the inner strength to make the changes needed to adapt to a new environment and to become the person you are yet to become.

DIMINISHING LANGUAGE DIFFICULTIES IN THE UNITED STATES

Jessie Chang
Taiwan

"Ring . . . ring . . . ring!" After the tenth ring, the phone stopped ringing. During those ten rings, I struggled to pick up the phone receiver, but couldn't do it. After all, it was only my second day in the United States, and I was alone in my friend's house for the first time since my arrival. What if the caller had been an American? I would never have been able to understand him or respond to him. Have you ever had such a fear?

A language phobia is only one of the many kinds of problems that the brand new foreigner faces here. Language difficulties will probably be the very first problems that you will need to confront, and the most all-pervasive and difficult ones to overcome. Communicating comfortably with English-speaking people will help you adapt to life in the United States. Learning how to diminish language difficulties will not necessarily be the most important thing for you to learn here, but by doing so you will more easily move among Americans and accomplish your goals in the United States.

Strategies for Improving Your English

How can you most efficiently get used to the American way of speaking English? First of all, you must accept that it takes time. The big words here are PRACTICE, PRACTICE, and still more PRACTICE! Such practice takes many different forms.

Perhaps the most passive and comfortable way is watching TV programs. It's low-to-no cost, convenient, and varied in its subject matter. It is more conducive to a quick understanding of spoken English than almost any other activity. It is also available most hours of the day or night. Ask your friends or neighbors for suggestions. What are their favorite programs? Why do they like them? What channels are the programs on? Try to choose programs that feature well-educated people who speak "standard" American English. Talk shows, news programs, and soap operas are often good choices. On other programs, you will learn how average Americans speak, some of whom are blue-collar workers or ethnic minorities. Along with language exposure, you will learn about American customs, values, and attitudes.

Listening to the radio is also a good activity, although you are missing the visual effects of what you are hearing. On the other hand, listening to the radio can help you concentrate all of your attention on how people speak: their pronunciation, their choice of words, and their sentence structure. This kind of concentration will rapidly increase your speed in comprehending the spoken language. It will also help you with those telephone calls.

More active and nerve-racking is talking to American friends and neighbors. Take every chance to practice by speaking English with your friends, acquaintances, and even strangers in the supermarkets, libraries, banks, and wherever else you might find yourself. The more you practice, the more you will learn and improve. "Practice makes perfect," says the American proverb.

Another approach to learning English is to read newspapers, books, and magazines. Local newspapers are good because they also keep you up to date on what's occurring in your area. Magazines which fall into your areas of interest are wonderful sources of entertainment and study.

Finally, many people who learn English as a second language rarely speak English at home. Those of us who live at home with our families have to go outside to find people with whom to practice English. Overcome your shyness and place yourself in various areas of the English-speaking community. This may be a new experience for you, but it is necessary. Schools, churches, and clubs are all good environments in which to practice your English and decrease problems of switching from your native language to English and vice versa. Take advantage of living in America, where it is easier to learn correct American English. Don't waste the opportunity.

One Last Suggestion for Improving Your English: Most foreigners depend too much on their bilingual dictionaries. Your bilingual dictionary cannot possibly give you the true meanings of all the words that you need to learn. What are the differences between *friend* and *acquaintance, equal* and *egalitarian, spiritual* and *religious,* and *empathy* and *sympathy?* What does *commitment* mean exactly? How do you use it in a sentence? Are you a *committed* person?

A good English-English dictionary will be of use in these areas. Two are especially good: *Longman's Dictionary of Contemporary English* and *Oxford Advanced Learner's Dictionary of Current English.* If these dictionaries are too difficult for you, look up the word in your bilingual dictionary as well and compare the definitions. Look at the word in context, that is, in a sentence of its own. You may find a big difference between what your bilingual dictionary and your monolingual one say. Practice making sentences and check them with an American to see if you understand how they are used.

Pointers on Variations in American English

Through your contact with different people each day, you'll hear many variations of speech. Professors and instructors, for example, often speak differently from supermarket clerks and factory workers; doctors often speak differently from gas station attendants. These variations result from different social, cultural, and educational levels.

Regional Differences: Differences can be found in the pronunciation, grammar, and vocabulary of people from different areas of the United States. Bostonians would say *Haavaad* for *Harvard*, while Milwaukeeans might say *warsh* for *wash*. Southern Californians would say "It's a nice day, *huh?*" instead of "It's a nice day, isn't it?" and when is a *frying pan* a *skillet*, or a *drinking fountain* a *bubbler?*

Social Differences: A person's English reflects his education and social class. There are also differences of sex, occupation, and neighborhood. Students speak differently with fellow students than with their teachers or parents. In the United States we hear slang everywhere. On campus, you'll hear students asking each other: "What's up?" "How's it goin'?" and saying, "Hey, take it easy!" Then there are the so-called four-letter words or dirty words. Examples of these I can't tell you, but then I probably don't have to because you have already been exposed to them, no doubt.

Standard versus Non-Standard English: Even though the United States is supposed to be a highly literate society, some people sound illiterate. Well-educated people normally speak standard English. Uneducated people have limited vocabularies and use more slang and vulgar expressions. It is sometimes difficult to know what they are talking about since they seem to slur words or use expressions which you can't find in your dictionary. Yet a linguist would make no judgments but would say that all dialects are valid forms. In fact, if a non-standard dialect were used by a majority of the educated leaders of the society, soon their dialect would become the standard, and the standard dialect would become the non-standard form.

One special dialect is called Black English. It tends to be difficult for outsiders to understand, for the pronunciation, grammar, and especially the vocabulary are different from standard English. Black English has had a profound influence on the way in which many Americans talk. You will hear words like *"funky"* and sentences like *"I ain't got no time"* in their spoken English and in their song lyrics. You may even be listening to some yourself now.

Although the differences between the two dialects are great, a writer named Sandra Haggerty wrote an article called "On Digging the Difference" for the *Los Angeles Times* in which she acknowledged the differences in language but stressed the feelings and actions common to all people, no matter what their language.

> *For some blacks and some whites (notice the infamous all has been omitted) it is not a matter of you say e-ther and we say i-ther, but rather:*
> *. . . You kiss your children, and we give 'em some sugar . . . .*
> *You cook a pan of spinach, and we burn a mess of greens.*
> *You wear clothes, and we wear threads . . . .*
> *You call the police, and we drop a dime.*

You say wow! We say ain't that a blip.
You care, love and hurt, and we care, love and hurt.
The differences are but a shade.

Finding out about all of these differences is fun and enriching. It's all part of the experience of living in a country like the United States. You will soon find yourself communicating with peoples of diverse ethnic and language backgrounds here. Remember my fear of answering the phone during my second day in the country? I'm no longer afraid (well, maybe just a little nervous) when I make my own phone call or simply answer the phone these days. I'm there with a "Hello!" and ready to handle whatever comes next.

DEALING WITH OUR GHOSTS OF THE PAST

Kim Lang Pu
Cambodia

Memories of people, events, and experiences from your past are sometimes pleasant; others haunt you with nightmarish feelings and anxieties: sometimes regret, sometimes longing, sometimes rage.

Some of us are refugees from war-torn countries. Although we are building a new life in America, we live in two different worlds. Even though life seems calm and predictable and the tragedies of war distant, we live in America by day and in our pasts by night. Few Americans have a sense of our pasts, and this ignorance produces in us a sense of isolation and unreality.

What has occurred to Cambodians like me has occurred in similar ways to Vietnamese, Laotians, Iranians, Salvadorans, and Nicaraguans. Names and places change, but the tragedies are the same. In April of 1975, the *Khmer Rouge* (Communist nationals) took over my homeland of Cambodia. Communist soldiers moved from house to house and ordered people to leave their possessions, their homes, and their neighborhoods.

I remember clearly the night when it happened to my family. The *Khmer Rouge* soldiers surrounded our house, entered, and accused my father of being a wealthy man and of wanting to escape to Thailand. We began to cry. It was clear that they were going to take him away. As they were leaving, one of them told us that if we didn't stop crying, they would be back to take us too. We tried to stop crying, but we couldn't hold back our tears.

Then they were gone, and my father with them. Fear gripped our hearts, and we cried together. That night we didn't sleep at all and hardly spoke of the unspeakable: that our father was gone and would never return. We never saw him again. We heard later that he had been interrogated, tortured, and shot.

The next morning, large groups of soldiers came to our house and took all our personal belongings, especially gold and clothing. The soldiers marched us and many others off into the countryside. On the way, entire families were murdered if they failed to move fast enough or if they complained. Still others were massacred for no reason at all. The deaths or suffering of individual human beings didn't seem to count for much.

Once in the countryside, the soliders segregated husbands, wives, and children. My own family was split up into separate work groups and living quarters. They placed my brothers and sisters with families who treated them like animals. I was lucky enough to be able to stay with my mother, for she was weak and unable to work. Even though I was only twelve, I did her job as well as my own.

All the members of my family were watched day and night for signs of foreign behavior. Even though we had been born and raised as Cambodians, we were considered to be foreign since we were ethnic Chinese. Our neighbors, an entire family, were killed for speaking in what the guards believed to be a Vietnamese accent. Others were bound, blindfolded, and dragged to the edge of pits and hit with heavy instruments, such as hoes or thick bamboo poles. Their blood reddened the earth. Some were not yet dead when the bulldozers pushed the earth over their bodies. The memory of it all filled our hearts and minds and continues to haunt us even now.

The rest of us spent a lot of time undergoing political and ideological indoctrination, which included poisonous ideas which were meant to undermine the careful training that our parents had given us. Both boys and girls were subjected to military conscription as early as the age of twelve. Parents lost control over their children's destinies as well as their hearts. All of us were forbidden to dance, read books, or take part in any philosophical, political, and cultural discussions.

During the day we cleared whole tracts of land, planted the new fields with rice, and did whatever the soldiers told us to do. We worked on and on, without complaint. At mealtime they fed us a small bowl of thin rice gruel and, on rare occasions when we were lucky, small amounts of fish or vegetables. We were always hungry. Anyone who collapsed from hunger or exhaustion or broke a rule faced immediate execution. Starving workers who were caught eating the dead bodies of people who had been executed faced the worst executions of all. For them there were special tortures. They were buried in the ground up to their shoulders and beaten to death . . . slowly.

People tried to escape. They swarmed out of the war zones into the unknown. Some were caught and executed; others died of starvation. Some wore no clothing and could not protect their bodies from mosquitoes and other parasites; others got malaria or suffered from bloody diarrhea, fever, and dizziness. With no medicine available to them, many died in their attempts to escape. Some were fortunate enough to make it to special camps where they were fed and clothed. They began to dream of the day when the horrors would finally be over. Little did they know that they would find little of personal value or meaning in the months and years to come or that they would not be part of their nation's reconstruction or its future.

As you can imagine, these experiences and memories have been so dreadful that those of us who lived through them cannot forget. Some of the wounds are beginning to heal, but others are still festering. They are sure to leave permanent emotional scars on our psyches.

Yet life must go on. Accepting this fact is the first step toward dealing with our ghosts of the past. Some of us have tried to leave them behind but have found it impossible. Perhaps our task should not be to forget the ghosts of the past but to accept them and move on by focusing on the present and the future. For whatever reason, we are the ones who made it out of hell alive. It's our special task to proceed with our lives in the present, even though we cannot completely forget the past. Our energies should focus on the future, individually and together, so that we can contribute to a world where these atrocities must never occur again.

RAISING A FAMILY IN THE UNITED STATES
(Cultural Conflict and Child Abuse)

Phu D. Nguyen
Viet Nam

The United States has historically been a haven for immigrants seeking a brighter future and freedom from oppression. Since April of 1975, waves of Indochinese, principally Vietnamese, have added new threads to the rich tapestry of American society.

They came to a new life in a strange country where they had no jobs or money and knew little of the language. Little more than ten years later, they have found themselves jobs, have earned some money, and have learned quite a bit of the language. Now new difficulties face them: the Americanization of their children, the increasing independence of their wives, and the strangeness of American society and culture.

In particular, child abuse is on the rise in Vietnamese homes and can be directly traced to the differences between authoritarian Vietnamese values and practices and the less authoritarian American ones. In Vietnamese homes, family relationships are highly structured, and the father's decisions are to be respected and followed; he is truly the head of the household. His wife is expected to be second to her husband and not to undermine his authority; she is expected to rear the children, while the father makes the decisions concerning the children's education and careers. He is the disciplinarian. Hitting and spanking children are considered normal disciplinary measures, even when the children are in their teens. In much the same way, older brothers and sisters often have considerable influence and authority over their younger brothers and sisters.

Both parents work hard to protect their children from the outside influences that they think are harmful. Compared to American children, Vietnamese children gain their independence at a very late age, especially the girls. Children are expected to obey and respect their parents and are taught to follow orders without complaint. They are not supposed to express their emotions or their feelings in front of people from outside the family. For these reasons, Americans often think of the Vietnamese as passive and lacking in initiative and creativity.

Once the children begin to attend American schools, some real problems begin to develop. It is easy to understand why child abuse has risen among the Vietnamese in the United States. The children learn American ways at school. They watch their American classmates become more independent and so they openly rebel. Their teachers also encourage them to speak up and to become more American. They adjust quickly, especially the younger ones.

When they go home, their parents are still very Vietnamese. They haven't so easily adapted to American life. The older the parents are, the more difficult it is for them to adjust. A gap between parents and children develops and continues to widen. Even more difficult to bridge is the gap between a Vietnamese-born parent and an American-born child.

Children often begin to defy their parents. The parents react by increasing the amount of discipline and punishment, and the children rebel all the more. The more frustrated the parents become, the more abusive their punishments. Tempers get out of control, and suddenly a child is physically abused.

The pressures on the father are especially great since the mother is slowly gaining more independence and is less inclined to follow all his wishes. The growing independence of the wives undermines the husband's self-image and his ability to deal with difficulties. He often feels powerless and, as a result, becomes more authoritarian.

Language and body language also contribute to the conflict. The children generally pick up English quickly, while the parents struggle and never speak it quite like native Americans. At home the parents want their children to speak Vietnamese, and at school their teachers and peers require that they speak English.

As far as body language is concerned, some gestures used in American culture are considered bad, even obscene in Vietnamese culture. Crossing your first two fingers means good luck in English, but it is vulgar and unacceptable to Vietnamese, especially if it is done by girls. Vietnamese parents would be horrified if they saw their son or daughter use that gesture.

Eye contact also means two different things to Vietnamese and Americans. Americans believe that not to look someone directly in the eyes means that you can't be trusted or that you have something to hide. Vietnamese, on the other hand, believe that looking someone straight in the eyes, especially if that person is a parent, teacher, or boss, indicates disrespect and rudeness. Usually the Vietnamese will, when speaking to a person in authority, look down and only occasionally glance up.

New pressures from the impact of a new culture can cause conflict within a family. With understanding and a willingness to be flexible and less rigid and restrictive, Vietnamese parents can avoid the tragedies of child abuse. Some boundaries have to be set, understood, and agreed upon by both parents and children as to what areas of family life will remain traditionally Vietnamese and what areas will accommodate American ways.

CHAPTER 8
SUCCEEDING ACADEMICALLY

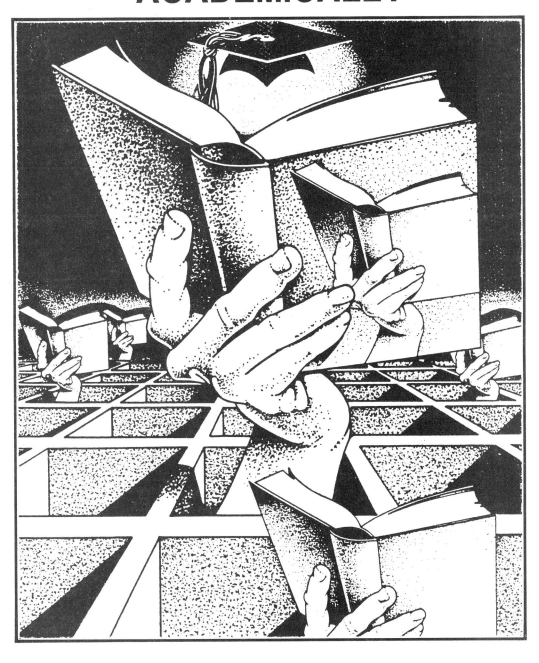

8. INTRODUCTION

A good education is invaluable in many ways; it enriches lives and leads to better jobs and higher salaries. Attending college or university in the United States will help you get that all-important education. In the process, you will be making major decisions for perhaps the first time in your life.

To make good decisions, you must take the initiative and ask questions in order to get the information that you need. You will be the one who decides what your course of study will be and how best to tackle the challenges that lie ahead. Most of your teachers will expect you to accomplish all assignments given. If you can't, you will need to see them in order to get some special help. Although they won't stand over your shoulder or seek you out, they will usually be glad to sit down with you and help you with any questions or difficulties.

Whether you want it to do so or not, an American education will force you to become more independent in your life. You can't afford to procrastinate or to take the easy way out. As the famous English biologist and educator, Thomas Henry Huxley, said in the latter part of the 19th century:

> *"Perhaps the most valuable result of all education is the ability to make yourself do the thing you have to do, when it ought to be done, whether you like it or not; it is the first lesson that ought to be learned; and however early (a person's) training begins, it is probably the last lesson he learns thoroughly."*

The sooner you learn to make your own decisions and to carry out what is required to get a good education in the United States, the sooner you will be on the road to accomplishing your educational goals and to becoming a mature and independent person.

SUCCEEDING ACADEMICALLY
(Ten Keys to Academic Success)

Gigi Kwok
and
Thomas K. C. Yuan
Hong Kong

We foreign students attend American colleges to gain knowledge, develop needed skills or techniques, and explore possible career goals. In addition, we acquire knowledge through contact with others in this multicultural society and learn how to take care of ourselves and make our own decisions. Still, our primary goal in an American college or university is, first and foremost, academic success. This means achieving a high level of scholastic learning and a grade point average (G.P.A.) to match.

The American educational system and its underlying philosophy, however, might be quite different from what you are used to in your homeland. If that is the case, a set of workable strategies will help you open the door to academic achievement in much the same way as an appropriate set of keys helps you open a locked door. The following strategies are the ones that worked for us. Perhaps they can work for you, too.

The first strategy in achieving academic success is to **establish a set of long range and short range goals.** You'll need to do some serious thinking in order that you might work with confidence to arrive at goals that are realistic and achievable. It also means that you'll want to consult your college bulletin and/or handbook in order to see what is needed to accomplish these goals. Goals enable you to fully develop your abilities yet help you to understand and accept your own limitations. It would be tragic if your potential abilities could not be fully developed either as a result of unchallenging, inadequate goals or as a result of goals set too high, so challenging that they are basically unattainable. Having realistic goals means you will choose well from among the great feast of classes offered at most American colleges and universities in order to work with confidence toward a chosen career or field of study.

With a good set of goals in hand, you will be more likely to **persevere even when the going gets tough.** A favorite Chinese fable concerns an old man who decided to remove a mountain because it blocked the way between two villages. While people in both villages laughed at him and called him crazy, he continued to move rocks and dirt day in and day out. He knew that he would succeed if he just kept at it. Because the mountain was very high and he was very old, he arranged for his sons and grandsons to complete the task should he be unable to. Like the old man, you, too, can achieve any goals you set your mind to. All you need is the same determination to see a goal through to completion. Unlike the old man, however, no one can achieve academic success for you. You will have to do all of the work yourself.

Perseverance, in fact, involves the willingness to **put in the work necessary to achieve your goal.** It has been said that success is 95% perspiration (hard work) and 5% inspiration (ability). Student A might be more intelligent than student B, but if he never works hard, he will not achieve the kind of success he desires. Even though student B might be less intelligent than student A, if he makes a consistent effort he is likely to surpass student A. An English proverb tells us, "If a man has a talent and does not use it, he has failed. If he has a talent and uses only half of it, he has partly failed. If he has a talent and learns somehow to use the whole of it, he has gloriously succeeded and won a satisfaction and a triumph few men know." Talent in conjunction with hard work is unbeatable.

Now comes a word of warning. Should you do well in the first part of a semester or quarter, do not take success for granted. Rather you should **maintain an even pace of consistent, dedicated effort throughout.** Aesop's fable concerning the race between the hare and the tortoise illustrates this strategy well. The hare, who began the race at high speed and looked like an easy winner, took a nap in the middle of the race, while the tortoise, who started slowly but maintained a consistent pace from beginning to end, won the race handily. The moral of the story is that "slow and steady" wins in the end. "Slow and steady" requires self-motivation and self-direction, for no one will tell you when to study, what to study, or how to study while you are in the United States. It's all up to you. Although the television and telephone will sometimes distract you and difficult assignments frustrate you, remember to keep up a steady effort.

To help yourself do this, **budget your time** by setting a work schedule for yourself. In this way, you will get all your work done and still have time to relax and have a little fun, too, since "all work and no play makes Jack (anyone) a dull boy (or girl). Because American instructors are generally quite time-conscious, make sure that all assignments are completed with care and turned in on the appropriate due-dates. Budgeting your time will also help you be on time for classes and lectures.

Up until now, the concern has been out-of-class preparation and conduct. What about in-class conduct? Just doing your homework is not enough. Except for large, formal lecture classes, be prepared to **contribute thoughtfully in class discussions, and ask questions when you don't understand.** For many of us, active in-class behavior runs counter to our upbringing. In our school days back home, students were expected to listen, not speak up. In fact, it often seemed as though the instructors there often preferred talking to the walls rather than to the students. Just the opposite is true of American instructors. Most even welcome students during their conference hours; this offers the student an opportunity to form a closer working relationship with the instructor. It is a time to clarify the instructor's expectations and to iron out any problems or misunderstandings concerning the course.

You may discover by talking to your instructor, or through some other means, that a needed study skill is weak or nonexistent. Perhaps poor note-taking skills prevent your taking adequate notes in a lecture class, underdeveloped reading skills keep you from fully understanding course content, or poor writing skills prevent the clear expression of your ideas on an essay test. In the face of such a discovery, you should **find out how your college or university can help you.** Do they have a learning skills laboratory or center? Are programs that help improve study habits available? Is there a tutorial service of any kind? These are some of the many services that most schools offer their students; take advantage of them.

Sometimes, however, suggestions and help from new friends can help most of all. Try to **make friends** with American students or other foreign students who have been here a while and who have gone through what you are now experiencing. Talk to them, go places with them, and study with them. Not only will this help you understand how others achieve academic success, but it will also make your academic experience more pleasurable.

When all else fails, remember to **be flexible.** If you are not getting the desired results or are suffering from a bit of homesickness, stop for a moment and observe yourself. Know that whatever you are feeling is normal and that others are probably feeling the same way you are. If your problem is the difference in educational styles or systems, you must soon realize that the American system will not change or go away. You are the one who will have to change and readjust yourself to the system.

A final strategy is to keep in mind always that **you, and you alone, are responsible for your academic success.** Many foreign students don't realize this immediately and continue to think that it is the instructor's responsibility. The sooner you take full responsibility for your learning experience, including the failures, the sooner academic success will be yours.

Toward that end, you have been offered this set of ten key strategies which have been designed to help you open the door to your academic achievement. Will you take them and use them well? If you do, we congratulate you in advance on achieving a hard-won goal—academic success—and a bright future in the making.

GETTING AROUND YOUR CAMPUS

Rene Arregoces
Colombia
Eva Gomez
Venezuela
Setyabudi Pratadja
Indonesia

Today, or maybe tomorrow, many of you will experience what I have already experienced. On my first day as a foreign student, I felt lost in a multitude, timid and unsure of what to do and where to go.

I felt conspicuous and self-conscious because of my heavily accented English. It was a confusing situation which I was sure most people here would never have understood. I thought that I could overcome these feelings by myself, but I did need some assistance along the way. Fortunately, people wanted to give me a hand in my adjustment to life here; they are ready to give you a hand, too.

The Foreign Student Advisor's Office and the Campus Center

Two of the special people at my college were the Foreign Student Advisor and the Student Activities Officer in our campus center. The Foreign Student Advisor and his secretary gave me some excellent advice on my immigration and monetary difficulties. They also helped me find my way around the campus and suggested that I explore the campus center first.

I took their suggestion and went to the campus center, known on some campuses as the student union. In the campus center at my college I found information about lockers, student identification cards, student handbooks, athletic eligibility, and student clubs. I noticed that this was the place where students congregated, relaxed, and even studied. It also had a cafeteria and a little cafe and lounge area. Most campus centers and student unions do.

There I also picked up an extra campus map; I decided to explore my campus. These are the places that I discovered and learned something about: the counseling office, the library, the bookstore, the college safety office or police department, and the health services center or campus clinic.

The Campus Counseling Office

Most American colleges and universities have counselors to help students make career decisions and face academic problems. Your school is probably no exception. In fact, it probably has an excellent counseling team to help you.

A counselor, if consulted with proper expectations, will be of immeasurable help to you in your academic life here. The counseling center is also the place where you can often find a reference library of college and university catalogues and information brochures, as well as applications for such tests as TOEFL, SAT, and GRE.

A counselor's job is to help you choose the right classes, arrange your schedule, and even decide on a major or a lifetime career. Feel free to ask questions; they are eager to answer your questions, as long as they are academic ones and as long as you have carefully prepared them.

When you have personal problems with homesickness, friends, and other matters, you may see your Foreign Student Advisor. In case of serious problems, you should see one of the school psychologists because they deal more with the student's personal, social, and learning problems than the academic counselors do.

The Campus Library

In addition to the counseling office, most colleges have fine libraries which help students, staff, and faculty do research more conveniently and efficiently. Besides a wide variety of books, you can also find pamphlets; domestic and international newspapers and magazines; audio-visual materials such as records, cassettes and videotapes; art prints; circulating encyclopedias; and coin-operated typewriters and copy machines.

You are encouraged to study individually or in groups in the library because it usually has a good atmosphere for studying. In fact, according to a recent survey on my campus, most students preferred to study in the library rather than in their own homes or apartments. It is also advisable for you to become familiar with the public library nearest your apartment, where you can sometimes acquire more information or a more complete set of certain sources. Whichever library you are exploring, request a library card at the circulation desk. Evidence of enrollment in your college is usually required.

The Campus Bookstore

Find out where your campus bookstore is located as soon as possible. It is a perfect place to find not only books but also other helpful articles. When you go inside the bookstore, you usually have to leave your books at the door while you shop. In the bookstore, you will find an excellent variety of books, not only for your classes, but also for your pleasure and interest, such as cooking, fiction, comic, and sports books. Your campus bookstore may also order books for you directly from the publisher.

Although book costs vary, you can generally expect to pay from $75.00 to $200.00 per semester for all of your textbooks and supplies. Of course, the cost depends on the courses you're taking and the supplies that you need. Once you have bought all of your books, save the receipt and do not mark in the books until you are absolutely sure that you do not need to exchange them or return them. If you do this, you will be eligible for a refund if you need one. Once you know that you are going to use the book for the semester, put your name and phone number in it, but not your address. At the end of the semester, do not throw away your books, for you can usually get money back by selling the books to the bookstore. If they are in good condition, both hardbacks and paperbacks will bring you about 50% of the original cost.

In the bookstore you can also find supplies for such specialized classes as art, music, and accounting. There are all kinds of paper supplies, pencils, stamps, cards to send to friends and family back home, decals for your car, T-shirts and shorts, as well as candy. As you can see, the bookstore is a place which offers a lot more than just books for your classes. The cashiers are usually ready to help you. Make sure that you find out when the store is open.

College Safety Office

The college safety office or police department is usually where you can get your parking permit; it depends on the campus. If you have a car and don't have a parking permit, you will probably get what I got last semester: lots of parking tickets. These cost money, so get yourself a parking permit. It's cheaper and more efficient in the long run. Fees vary according to school; at mine they cost $20 a semester, whereas at some schools students have to pay as much as $95.

One important piece of advice: always lock your car. The college or university is not responsible for stolen items or damage to your car. Therefore, do not leave valuable items in plain view. Put them in the trunk or under the seat. Do not panic if you leave your car keys inside your car, or if you have a flat tire or dead battery. The safety office on your campus is usually ready to help you with all of these problems.

The Health Services Center

If you don't have your own doctor, and most foreign students do not have one, this office can be very helpful to you. It provides nursing services, and usually a physician is available too. If you have a fever or an eye infection, for example, the doctor will examine you and give you a prescription. Also available are aspirins, band-aids, and good advice, according to your need. A special fee is usually paid at registration to cover various medical expenses for an entire semester. Again, check on what hours they keep.

In conclusion, whatever your need or desire, never feel afraid to ask. There is always a place where you can get what you need. The information in this article is of a general nature, for each campus is slightly different. However, following the itinerary given in this article, you should be able to take quite a pleasant and informative tour of your new campus.

ARTICLE 8.3

PRODUCING MORE IN LESS TIME

Saba Syed Hafeez
Pakistan

From the moment the foreigner arrives in the United States, he will hear such expressions as *"Time waits for no man," "Time flies,"* and *"Time is money."* Time . . . time . . . time! What is this American obsession with time? Americans seem to consider time their most prized possession, as if it were something to be "saved," "spent," "lost," or "wasted." These expressions will haunt you in the United States unless you get into step and learn to manage your time wisely and effectively.

Do you already feel frustrated by the fast pace of life here, where each moment seems programmed? Are you encountering common American problems regarding time management, such as too many things to do, too little reward for hard work, tight schedules, work turned in late, and procrastination? Even though Americans have lived with these problems most of their adult lives, they seem to have no easier time of it than you or I. They are just more accustomed to it.

An American time management consultant, Alan Lakein, wrote a best-seller called *How to Get Control of Your Time and Life.* It is considered by some to be the best book written on the subject. Here are some of his time management techniques which might be useful to you.

Whatever you want to do, set goals. Then ask yourself if these goals are really important to you. Once you have decided that they are, decide which ones are the most important and rank them. Choose activities for each of these goals and try to do something each day in order to accomplish them. For example, if a driver's license is one of your goals, make a list of activities which you need to do to accomplish this goal. One activity might be to practice your driving a half an hour daily.

Review your goals and activities. Every night give yourself five to ten minutes to make your plans for the next day. Make a list of things to do in order of importance. In the morning, take a few more minutes to revise and review your list. Don't make your schedule too tight. Allow some time for emergencies and intrusions. Always allow more time for your important jobs.

Categorize your jobs so that you can do a number of errands on the same route. Accommodate your time to schedules of others. If you have to discuss something with a teacher or friend, schedule your time with them at their convenience.

Here are some refinements on the above suggestions:

1. The better you plan, the better you will do. So don't be afraid of "wasting" time on planning, for you will be "saving" time in the long run.

2. Try to stick to your list. Do one thing at a time in the order that you have set. Check

things off the list as you do them. At the end of the day, you may congratulate yourself on having done all your jobs or at least the most important ones. Now give yourself a treat.

3. Don't worry about the time spent on activities out of your control and not on your list, but try to say "no" nicely and diplomatically to someone who asks you to do something which has little importance for you.

4. Consider "waiting time" as "gift time" to relax, make plans, or do something that you wouldn't otherwise do. Waiting time occurs in supermarket lines, in class registration lines, at bus stops, and at the bank.

5. Try to avoid watching TV altogether, or watch no more than one or two of your favorite programs daily. Make one choice the international and national news and the other a free choice.

6. Try as much as you can to be honest with yourself about how you use your time. Be strict with yourself when you break your rules.

7. Don't worry about unimportant jobs which you can't finish. Congratulate yourself on the important ones that you did accomplish.

Following these suggestions will help you break any habits of procrastination that you may have and help you realize that "procrastination is the thief of time." It will also help you use your time effectively and intelligently. In addition, you will gain control of your life and end up enjoying it more than before. You will now have less to worry about and more time for friends and fun!

Note: I would like to thank Alan Lakein for helping me "get control of my time and my life" as well as for giving me the opportunity to write an essay on a topic which interested me. For further reading on this topic, pick up his book, *How to Get Control of Your Time and Your Life,* published by Signet Publishers, from your local library or bookstore. It will be well worth your time and money!

CHAPTER 9
EARNING, BUDGETING, AND SPENDING SUCCESSFULLY

9. INTRODUCTION

"Though mothers and fathers give us life, it is money alone which preserves it," wrote Ihara Saikaku, a seventeenth-century Japanese writer. Few people around the world, then or now, would disagree with him, especially if they were new arrivals in a foreign country. In the United States, many of you will realize, perhaps for the first time in your lives, how crucial money is to your survival and well-being. Your sources of money will be your lifelines, whether those sources be funds that your families send you, savings that you've brought with you, scholarships or grants that you've won, or wages that you earn.

Although being here will offer you daily opportunities to learn to earn, save, and spend your money wisely, reading the three articles in this chapter will set you in the right direction. The first discusses the process of finding and keeping a job in the United States, the second introduces ways of managing your money, and the third suggests tips on ways to spend that money well.

FINDING A JOB

Wai Hing Yip
Malaysia

Everyone wants and needs money, right? But how does one go about getting it? One thing you could do is try for a scholarship, but that takes time, effort, and a certain amount of good luck. Or you could rob a bank, but that is dangerous and could get you into trouble. Most likely, you will decide to do what most people do who need and want money: get a job.

Foreign students have a certain number of problems facing them when they try to find employment in the United States, especially while attending school. However, there are ways of being successful in your search for part-time or temporary employment. Here are some guidelines to help you locate a job, prepare your job application, get hired, and keep your job once you have it.

Getting Permission to Work

If you are a student with an F-1 visa, you must get a work permit before starting to work. There are always some people who, for whatever reasons, work illegally. They run the risk of being caught and, in some cases, deported. As a result, it is much better to do it legally.

Before you consider working off-campus, look for an on-campus job. In any case, you will need the approval of your foreign student advisor, so first go to the Foreign Student Advisor's office on campus with a prepared statement of good reasons in support of an application for a work permit. You must be enrolled in a college or university for at least twelve units per semester and maintain a G.P.A. minimum of 2.00 or above in order to keep your work permit. You will then receive your permission to work.

Second, go to the United States Department of Immigration with the permission to work from your Foreign Student Advisor. Immigration personnel will issue an official working permit.

Finally, go to the Social Security Office to apply for a social security number. You must also bring along your international passport, Form 1-94, and all other documents of proof that you are a student at a local college or university.

Finding Job Information

On campus, you can go to the Job Placement Center. The people who work in that office can give you information on jobs that they know are available. If you are a permanent resident or refugee, you may join the federally funded College Study Program. Unfortunately, this program is not open to F-1 visa students.

Off campus, you can look in the classified ads in local newspapers, sign up at public or private employment agencies found in the yellow pages of the telephone book, or ask friends for introductions or suggestions.

Making a Good Impression at a Job Interview

The first thing you should do is to plan the answers to several possible questions which the interviewer may ask. Then you should carefully prepare what you are going to wear. Depending on the job, a man might want to wear a suit, a dress shirt, and a tie. A woman should wear conservative office clothes, such as a suit and higher-heeled shoes. Do not wear jeans or T-shirts. Be sure your hair is neat and tidy. And make sure that you arrive on time.

Earning a Salary

Although as a student you should work no more than twenty hours per week, you can usually earn the legal minimum wage or more. You may even be able to earn double pay when you work after regular working hours or on holidays and weekends. This, however, depends on your employer.

Keeping Your Job

First you have to be enthusiastic on the job. Show that you enjoy your work. Be responsible and always get your work done on time. You should also not be absent from work without a good reason. If you need to be absent, call your employer to let them know. Always be on time and do not leave early except by permission for special circumstances. In addition, it is important for you to be friendly and kind to your supervisors and other staff members in order to have good working relationships with them. Finally you should *always ask questions whenever you are in doubt.*

These steps and procedures should help you get a job and keep it while you study at a college or university in the United States. You will not only help make your financial ends meet, but you will also have an opportunity to improve your English by this kind of contact with other Americans. Even though you may not be immediately successful in your search for a job, keep trying until you reach your goal. You'll be glad you did.

ARTICLE 9.2

MANAGING YOUR MONEY

Dewi Gunawan
Indonesia

Are you trying to live on a limited budget? As a foreign student, I have had to be careful with how I spend my money. My parents send me a small amount of money every month which I have learned to manage successfully. I pay my bills and living expenses and put any money left over in a savings account.

One of the ways to manage a limited amount of money is to make a budget. When you make a budget, you list your expenses and compare them with your income. In my case, I made the following list of my regular monthly expenses and compared that with the $550 that I receive each month.

1. $220.00 for my share of the apartment rent. (I have two roommates.)

2. $150.00 for food, which I cook at home or eat in a restaurant.

3. $85.00 for telephone and transportation.

$95.00 is left over, and this money I save or use for extras like entertainment, haircuts, new clothing, new shoes, and miscellaneous items.

What if you find your expenditures are greater than your income? You need to reverse the situation. One thing which you can do is to try to limit or eliminate expenses. Here are some areas where I have cut expenses:

1. I no longer buy expensive make-up.

2. I cook most meals myself rather than eat out in restaurants. (I save the latter for special occasions.)

3. I eat more vegetables and rice than meat and fish. (Meat and fish are expensive.)

4. I look for inexpensive entertainment like tennis, swimming, visiting friends, baking, and watching T.V.

5. I share my apartment with two roommates so that I pay 1/3 the amount of rent I used to pay.

6. I often walk to school rather than drive my car. It's good exercise, refreshing (except on hot or rainy days), and economical. Besides, I never have parking worries when I walk.

Maybe you could try some of these yourself and then add some of your own ideas to the list.

One question you might be asking is, "What should I do if I run short of money?" A number of solutions will help you out of a tight bind:

- Perhaps there is an office on campus that offers small emergency funds to help students out.
- Sell your new or old merchandise at a local flea market.

- Borrow money from friends or relatives.
- Get a loan from the bank where you have an account.
- Limit your expenses (telephone, entertainment, clothes).
- Find a job.

As a foreign student who is far away from home, I have learned to budget my money well; I make my own decisions and take responsibility for those decisions. This has been an excellent opportunity to learn about my capabilities and strengths. I have also learned to make important choices. May managing your own money do the same for you!

BUYING WISELY IN
THE UNITED STATES

Yvonne Kang
Hong Kong

Are you looking for a new car or bargain-priced used car? How can you avoid being fooled or cheated by unscrupulous and overly clever salesmen? These and other questions will come to mind when you wish to buy not only automobiles but major appliances, clothing, and many daily necessities.

If you are a new foreign student in this country, you may be confused by the variety of products that you see advertised on television or hear about on the radio. You will also run into ads in newspapers, catalogs, phone books, and brochures in your mailbox. How are you going to choose the best products and make wise decisions on what to buy? The following are some basic techniques and ideas which will save you time and money and eliminate headaches.

How to Analyze Advertising

In this country, you can't escape advertising, which is so convincing that it makes everyone want to run out and buy the item immediately. How can you avoid falling into the trap?

First of all, don't believe everything that you see in ads because advertisers will use any trick to get your attention and increase sales. They will promote a product by using techniques to weaken your resistance. Avoid buying a product which you don't need, so that you won't feel disappointed later on. Therefore, you should watch out for empty promotional jargon like "Buy 2-for-1 sales" or "Buy one, and get one free." Many of these offers are simply not true; the seller is just making an offer that sounds better than it is. *Remember:* before you buy, read all the small print in ads because they are sometimes more important than the big bold print that catches your attention.

APPLIANCES

Where can you buy appliances? Appliances are very important because you can't live comfortably without them. Since you are a newly-arrived foreigner, appliances are sometimes included in your quarters and sometimes not. Make a list of appliances which you don't have, so that you will be able to decide what you need to purchase. For example, you may need a coffee maker, a toaster, an iron, a microwave oven, or a T.V. set. These appliances can be found in department, discount, or specialty stores, or even in your nearby supermarket. These stores often have sales, so watch for their advertisements in newspapers, catalogs, and your mailbox.

How to Buy Appliances

First, visit several large department or discount stores where they have a complete display of many kinds of appliances, and write down the model number and price of the appliance in which you are interested.

Second, look in the yellow pages of the telephone directory under the type of appliance, such as "Televisions" or "Electric Appliances." Then telephone these stores to learn the lowest price available. It might be worthwhile to spend more time and compare prices before making your purchase.

Third, be sure that you don't get cheated by salesmen who quote low prices and then switch the model on you. You should double check everything carefully. Whether you buy a large or a small appliance, service is also a very important consideration when the warranty has expired. Sometimes it is cheaper to throw away an inexpensive appliance than to have it repaired. Remember to keep the receipt as well as your warranty certificate when you buy any appliance, because the receipt showing the date of purchase is just as important as the warranty itself.

AUTOMOBILES

Which should you buy, a new or used car? Your budget should tell you which kind of car you can afford. If you decide on a new car, you probably have to buy from a dealer. Look around in your own community to get the lowest price.

How to Buy a New Car

The best technique for buying a new car is to select the style, make, size, color, and extra options, such as air conditioning and stereo, and then to shop among several dealers for the best price for the kind of car that you want. For instance, you may prefer a foreign car, but if you find an American-made car which has all the features that you want, and it is several thousand dollars cheaper, you may change your mind. Keep an open mind.

Before you decide on which car to buy, ask people you know about their car's performance, the mileage per gallon of gasoline, and general handling. It is also a very good idea to check consumer rating guides and automobile magazines. You can find these books and magazines in your nearby library.

Assuring Your Car's Performance

Check the car before you buy; always take it for a good test drive so that you can get an accurate feel of the vehicle's steering and braking systems and its general stability. Make sure that the test drive is long enough; don't take it during the evening or in bad weather — you may rush your inspection. Also make sure that the windshield wipers, headlights, heater, air conditioning, ventilation, radio, and other accessories are all in perfect condition.

After deciding on the car of your choice, you are ready to compare prices. In this way, you will not base your buying decision on the price alone.

The salesmen may use a sales technique called "low-balling," which is to quote a price so low that it will make you stop shopping. Be careful! There may be a trick. Perhaps the car doesn't have the options that you expected; or it could be the wrong model. Watch out for the salesmen who make only spoken commitments for "unbelievably low prices" on new cars. They may withdraw their commitments just as you are about to sign the paper on the pretext that the sales manager would not approve the price that he quoted. *Remember:* Before you sign anything, make sure that you understand the documents, including the warranty, because it tells you how much free service you can expect if something goes wrong with the car. You should always remember that in the United States you can only depend on a written warranty. Do not believe any spoken ones.

How to Buy a Used Car

In addition to following some of the advice given under the section "How to Buy a New Car," you have further considerations to make.

First, a good person from whom to buy a used car is one of your friends or relatives; you may get a better price because you know them well and you are less likely to be cheated or disappointed.

Second, you might consider buying a used car from a stranger. Always remember to have the car checked by an expert for possible problems; it is your responsibility to have it fixed if something goes wrong since you have no warranty from a friend, a relative, or a stranger.

You might also call the National Highway Traffic Safety Administration's Office of Consumer Service to get more car inspection information. Their toll-free number is 1-800-404-9393. Tell them the make, model, and vehicle identification number of the car. They will then tell you of any known factory defect recalls for the car. If the car that you are considering has such defects, be sure that the dealer has repaired the defects. If the car checks out well, then you can bargain with the owner for a lower price. Usually a private owner is easier to deal with than a car salesman. You can also find out the actual price of any car model or year by looking it up in the "Automobile Blue Book." This is the book used by car dealers to establish a selling price. You can ask to see a copy of this useful book at your public library.

Third, if you buy a used car from a new or used car dealer, don't believe everything that the salesman says. Check everything out carefully by following the procedure outlined above under "How to Buy a New Car."

Words of warning: Never accept a car without a test drive. If the car drive reveals problems, don't make the purchase unless the problems are fixed or the price is adjusted. Moreover, be sure to get a title that doesn't carry an unpaid loan.

CLOTHING
How to Buy the Right Clothes

Clothing plays a very important role in your life; clothes affect the way you look at yourself and the way you are looked at by others. If you shop wisely, you can own a wardrobe that looks as if you have spent a fortune, while it actually cost you much less. You *can* dress well on a small budget if you follow these important suggestions:

1. Do some comparison-shopping at home by using catalogs, newspaper ads, and magazines for ideas.
2. Go to stores and compare prices, quality, and sizes.
3. Choose the best quality that fits your budget.
4. Always check labels before you buy in order to consider the maintenance costs.
5. Be careful with the "sale" items because they are not always the best buys.
6. If you find an item which is appealing, keep in mind that sale items are final. Always try on garments before buying them.
7. Make sure you are buying the right item for the right occasion.

Many of the principles and suggestions made for purchasing appliances, automobiles, and clothing apply to most other purchases as well. The information provided is intended to help you avoid some of the more common mistakes. If you keep these helpful ideas in mind, you will soon become a skillful shopper.

As long as you shop in this way, you will not only save money, but also get more satisfaction out of the money that you spend. You may even want to purchase items which are not necessities but luxuries. Then it will be up to you and your budget. *Remember:* the contented buyer comes home happy with the thought that the purchases made are the right ones. Overall satisfaction with the product is the consumer's primary goal. You should be the one who has the control, not the advertiser or the merchant.

CHAPTER 10
AVOIDING TROUBLE AND TROUBLE-SHOOTING

10. INTRODUCTION

An old proverb says: "An ounce of prevention is worth a pound of cure."
Preventing trouble before it has a chance to occur is especially important
when you are living in a foreign country. The first article in this chapter,
written by a student of nursing, offers sound advice on how to stay healthy
and avoid unnecessary illness and medical expense.

Yet sometimes in spite of our best preventive measures, we find ourselves
involved in trouble that we had little or no chance to prevent. Automobile
accidents often fall into this category. The second article offers advice on
how to avoid an alcohol-related accident, while the third tells you what to
do in case an auto accident should occur.

Finally what should you do if you need emergency medical care as a
result of any kind of accident? The fourth article tells you what to do
immediately following an accident and what to expect if you find yourself
needing emergency medical care.

STAYING HEALTHY

Hideyuki Tanaka
Japan

Most of you in the United States are no doubt happy and excited about the new experiences to come. You are also probably healthy and feeling good. You may think that you will never get sick here. The possibility of getting sick, however, is one of the obstacles facing every foreign student. The food, weather, and life style are all different from what you are used to, and you may come under a lot of stress because of these differences.

Staying healthy should be one of your most important goals. Using preventive measures is the best way to stay healthy and happy and avoid needless expenditure on health care.

Nutrition

The first step in the prevention of illness is good nutrition. The human body needs good fuel and building material. That means foods which provide proteins, carbohydrates, fats, vitamins, and minerals. Without proper nutrition, health cannot be maintained. Therefore you must watch the kind of food you put into your body.

You may be living alone here for the first time in your life. This means that you will be responsible for your own meals and nutrition and may even have to prepare your own food at home. Generally speaking, the average male college student between the age of 20 and 30 needs about 2800 calories for energy daily. Women in this age group usually require somewhat fewer calories, about 2100 daily. If you try to eat foods from the four basic food groups at every meal, you will probably come close to an ideal diet. The four food groups are the following:

1. Fresh Vegetables and Fruits

The members of this group are important sources of vitamins A, E, and C, as well as minerals and fiber. You need a continuous supply of vitamin C on a daily basis because it is not retained in your body as vitamins A and E are. Good sources of vitamin C are citrus fruits, melons, berries, broccoli, spinach, and tomatoes.

You also need frequent servings of deep-yellow or dark-green vegetables in order to get vitamins A and E and important minerals. It is better to eat unpeeled fruits and vegetables and those with edible seeds such as berries in order to get enough fiber, which will help you avoid the common American problem of constipation. Most natural foods which are unprocessed are rich in vitamins, minerals, and fiber. If you eat them fresh, either raw or slightly steamed, you will derive the most benefit from them.

2. Protein

Fifty-five grams of protein are needed daily for the average adult; this means about 25% of the diet should be protein. This group includes two kinds of protein. Animal proteins, such as milk, eggs, meat, and fish, are usually considered complete proteins. Plant proteins, such as soy-beans and legumes, are considered incomplete proteins. If you eat plant proteins, you can combine two kinds of foods, such as beans and wheat or beans and rice, to get as complete a protein as meat offers. These not only cost less but also contain less cholesterol than meats and fish. Organ meats and egg yolk contain higher levels of cholesterol than fish or poultry; so if you prefer animal proteins, most of them should come in the form of fish and poultry.

3. Grains and Carbohydrates

This group includes all whole grain products, such as wheat and rice. These foods, especially in their natural forms, are important sources of B-vitamins, which help you maintain a healthy nervous system when under stress, as well as minerals and iron. This group of foods is often refined and, in the process, loses much of its valuable vitamin and mineral content. Many American snacks and beverages, such as those luscious pastries, crispy cookies, tasty potato chips, refreshing soft drinks, wines, and beers are appealing, taste wonderful, but can do damage to your health in the long run. You must also be careful about the amounts you take in. Otherwise, you will become a victim of empty calorie foods: overweight and only half-healthy. It's better to eat a variety of fresh fruits, whole grains, and vegetables in order to get the calories that you need as well as those important vitamins and minerals.

4. Fats and Oils

Fats and oils have more than twice the calories of proteins, grains, or even sugars. If you eat extra fat, you will gain weight. The best sources of fat are unsaturated, such as vegetable oils, which are easily absorbed by your body and are also rich in vitamin E. All animal fats are saturated and, once you have eaten them, they wander around in your bloodstream, causing pile-ups and clotting of blood passages. Then problems such as heart trouble and strokes can more easily occur.

Besides these four food groups, water is very important for your health. You need at least six cups daily to maintain good health.

Now what about the preparation of your food? The simpler the preparation, the better the nutrition. Variety and moderation are always the keys to a good diet. You may want to eat out sometimes, but be sure to choose a good combination, and that means including a salad or fresh fruit.

Some students skip breakfast, because they don't have time. Actually, a good breakfast is more important than either of the other two meals. Those who eat a good breakfast will pay more attention in class, be more alert in their studies, and probably get better grades. If you are one of those who doesn't have time enough to eat a good breakfast, try to get up a little earlier.

At times you may feel that you do not have time to cook lunch or dinner. It's more convenient to buy canned foods, frozen foods, and T.V. dinners, not to mention those snack items from the vending machines. However, these foods have lost much of their nutritional value during the manufacturing process. Many of them have had colorings, flavorings, and preservatives added to them. Those additives may be harmful to your body. Why should you pay more to get junk foods than you do to get natural foods, especially since natural foods are better for your health? Remember, it's almost always better to eat foods prepared from scratch than to eat those that have been processed and prepared by a manufacturer!

Exercise

Besides proper nutrition, exercise is another way to keep healthy. Everyone knows that daily exercise can help you maintain good health. If you are interested in participating in an intramural sports program, you might join some individual sports which are offered year-round at your college or university. You should find a sport which you truly enjoy so that you can continue it on a regular basis. Otherwise, simply take walks or go jogging; it's inexpensive and anyone can enjoy these activities any time and any place, alone or with friends. Exercise not only benefits your body, but also helps relieve tension and fatigue.

Rest and Relaxation

It is normal for foreign students to experience homesickness and tension. This is the natural product of living in a new country and facing a different life style and set of customs. No one can avoid it, but you can learn how to deal with it. Here are some suggestions:

1. Talk out your problems with someone you trust. This will help relieve stress and allow you to see your anxiety from a different angle.
2. Learn to accept the things that you cannot change; work to change only the things that are changeable.
3. Work off tension with physical exercise when you are angry or upset.
4. Get a good night's sleep. Have a regular bedtime and try to get at least seven hours of sleep at night. Avoid staying up studying the whole night for a quiz the next day.
5. Give yourself time off. When you feel anxious and full of worries about something, read a good book, visit a friend, or go to the movies. This can help you catch your breath and come back to face problems with optimism and a fresh attitude.

As you can see, it is extremely important for foreign students always to maintain good health. You know that without good nutrition, proper exercise, and relaxation, your physical and mental well-being cannot continue. If you follow the simple advice just given, you will have a healthy and happy stay in the United States.

AVOIDING AN ALCOHOL-RELATED ACCIDENT

Yat C. Ho
Hong Kong

As soon as I got my driver's license here, I went out and bought my first car. A few days later, I was on my way to pick up a few friends to celebrate this. As I was driving along, I suddenly heard a thunderous sound in front of me. I slammed on my brakes. Then something hit me from behind ... I heard the noise of screeching wheels and a car moving away at top speed.

Splinters of glass were scattered all over the inside of my car; my head was throbbing. It slowly occurred to me that I had been in a car accident. The police and ambulance arrived at the scene about five minutes later. The driver of the first car had been seriously injured, for I vividly remember seeing blood coming from his ears. Later, the police caught the man who had hit me from behind. He had been driving under the influence of alcohol, a fairly common occurrence.

In the United States, everyone has a chance of being involved in an alcohol-related traffic accident at some time in his life. Now that you are living here, that includes you, too. The figures related to alcohol-related accidents are frightening. Approximately 25,000 human lives are snuffed out each year on American roads and highways, while 650,000 people are injured, some maimed and crippled for life.

All of us should try to understand the problem and be on our guard in order to avoid such an accident. To understand the problem, we should first become aware of the effects of alcohol on a driver. A clear mind, excellent reflexes, and good vision are all essential to being an alert and safe driver. Alcohol acts as a depressant on the central nervous system. It confuses your mind, slows your responses, and dims your vision. Therefore when you drink, you diminish your ability to make good judgments. You will relax and have a feeling of euphoria; you will not realize that you are not suitable to drive. Therefore, do not drink if you plan to drive.

Recently, a classmate of mine died in an accident. She and three friends were driving home around 2 A.M. after enjoying a few drinks at a party. Her boyfriend, who had drunk quite a bit, lost control of his car and crashed into a telephone pole. She went through the windshield, suffered brain damage, and died several days later. He was killed instantly.

What about accidents in which you haven't been drinking, but someone in another car has? If you want to avoid this kind of accident, try not to drive between 9 P.M. and 3 A.M., especially on weekends. It has been reported that at least 10% of all weekend drivers are illegally intoxicated, and as many as four out of every ten drivers drive under the influence of alcohol.

Another good practice is to wear seat belts, which is now the law in some states. Fortunately, I was wearing my seat belt the night I was hit. This prevented me from flying through the windshield.

We can also prevent accidents by practicing some simple rules. When you plan a party, you should be a responsible host. Instead of serving alcoholic beverages, serve soft drinks and juices as well. Never let your friends drive if you think they are drunk. You should make them stay or ask someone to drive them home. And never risk your life by getting in a car with someone who is drunk.

According to statistics, people between the ages of 16 and 24 represent only 20% of the licensed drivers in the United States. However, this is the same group which is involved in 42% of all alcohol-related fatal crashes. Some of us belong to this high-risk group. It is time to face the consequences of driving while under the influence of alcohol. So next time you drink, don't drive.

ARTICLE 10.3

DEALING SUCCESSFULLY WITH AN AUTO ACCIDENT IN AMERICA

Juili Chang
Taiwan

Nowadays in America, a car is just like one's feet. Everybody needs to know how to drive a car, just as we all need to know how to walk. Cars are so common and so much a part of our transportation here, especially in California, that if you know how to drive a car, you had better know what to do in case of an auto accident. No matter how carefully you drive, the other driver may cause an accident. The Immigration and Naturalization Service does not deport foreigners involved in accidents, but you could get embroiled in some legal problems. If you know what to do, you can usually avoid such problems.

Most people react with panic or even hysteria when they have an accident. This is unnecessary. Staying calm is essential. Following these instructions step by step will help you overcome your anxiety and stay calm.

First, as soon as the accident occurs, stop your vehicle. Most states require that you stop when you are in an accident that involves a pedestrian, a moving car, a parked car, or someone's property. If you drive away, you could be guilty of "hit and run." The penalties for this are severe: a fine or sometimes even jail.

Second, at the scene of the accident, do not volunteer any information about whose fault it was. Talk to your insurance agent, your lawyer, or both before accepting any blame. Don't agree to pay damages, and don't sign anything, except a traffic ticket which you will be required to sign in any case. Foreign students tend not to understand that a ticket has nothing to do with guilt or innocence. Always cooperate with the police officer investigating the case. Stick to the facts, and do not give opinions.

Third, exchange the following information with the other driver or drivers involved: names, addresses, telephone numbers, and driver's license numbers. Also exchange license plate numbers, and the color, year, make, and model of the cars. For example, you may have been driving a white 1983 Oldsmobile Omega with the license plate XTZ639, and the other driver may have been driving a blue 1974 BMW 2002 with the license plate MOJ119. Then exchange the names, addresses, and telephone numbers of your insurance companies.

Fourth, get the names, addresses, and phone numbers of any passengers in the cars and any other witnesses to the accident. Ask them to tell you what they saw and write everything down. In addition, write down the name and badge number of the police officer who is investigating the accident, and ask him where you can get a copy of the accident report. Make notes, too, on weather and road conditions and the exact time and place the accident happened. A word of warning: don't move any injured people. If you have a blanket or a coat, put it over them.

Finally, report your accident to your insurance agent as soon as possible. Your insurance agent will usually take care of everything for you.

ARTICLE 10.4

EXPERIENCING AN EMERGENCY WARD

Zusell Wong
Hong Kong

Imagine how you would feel if you were injured in an accident and needed emergency care. What if you were bleeding and unable to move? You would probably be afraid and panicky. Heart attacks, strokes, seizures, and various types of accidents, especially automobile accidents, can happen to anyone at any time in any place. It is important that you know what to do when someone's life is in danger. You, your family, or your friends may lose precious moments fumbling through the telephone book for the right phone number to call or deciding on the best ambulance service.

Lost moments or poor decisions can produce fatal results. It would be preferable to call **911,** a special emergency number which is in operation in more than 75% of the United States; this number will obtain immediate assistance from the police department, fire department, or emergency services of a hospital.

Americans as well as foreigners are generally inexperienced in handling emergencies. Because every minute counts once an emergency has occurred, quick and proper treatment are critical. Suppose that you or your friend were taken to an emergency ward of a hospital as a result of calling **911.** What would you face? How soon would they take care of you? Under what conditions? Who would treat you? And how well?

According to a recent survey, half of the patients who have been in an emergency ward were annoyed with the long wait and involved paper work. This often occurs because the hospital needs to know your medical history and the nature of the accident before they treat you; they also treat the most severely injured or seriously ill first, no matter who arrived first. Generally, doctors and nurses are on hand to take care of you, but you are sometimes treated by paramedics.

Here are four suggestions which will help you deal with emergencies as they occur:

First, get a health insurance plan as soon as possible. Medical bills are unbelievably high in the United States. Also, more and more hospitals require their patients to have health insurance before admitting them to the emergency room.

Second, become familiar with your local hospitals and emergency clinics. Where are they located, what kinds of equipment and services do they provide, and what are the qualifications of the emergency staff? If possible, visit your local hospital or emergency ward. Don't hesitate to ask questions of the staff or patients at the facility. Realize that sometimes differences in the quality of care among different emergency wards is found in the training of their personnel.

Third, know some first aid procedures, for these are invaluable when an emergency happens. One type of first aid is Cardiopulmonary Resuscitation (CPR), a technique used to help a heart attack victim start breathing and pumping blood again. Since heart attacks are the primary killer in the United States, it would be wise for everyone to learn CPR and other related techniques.

Fourth, when an emergency occurs, you should try to stay calm, so that you will be able to say what needs to be said and do what needs to be done.

I hope that you and your loved ones never find yourselves under emergency care. If you do, however, you now know exactly what to do and what to expect. Don't wait for something to happen; prepare yourself now.

CHAPTER 11
EXPLORING THE REST OF AMERICA

11. INTRODUCTION

Now that you've spent so much time and energy getting used to American life, struggling with the English language, making new friends, and accomplishing your academic and career goals, how about spending a little more time, energy, and money on fun and adventure?

Exploring some of America that you haven't seen yet is one of the best ways to have fun and adventure, and to enrich your American experience at the same time. The beauty of various wilderness areas is one of the most unique and precious treasures America has to offer you. In addition, you will find that every American city and region you visit affords many new cultural and recreational opportunities.

The two articles in this chapter offer you excellent suggestions, ideas, and encouragement on traveling around the United States. The first article helps you decide on a destination, plan an itinerary, choose your means of transportation, prepare what you need for the trip, and get the most from the experience once you're on the road. The second explores, in more poetic form, the special joys of camping in the United States. Wherever you decide to go and however you decide to do it, enjoy the cultural and recreational diversity of America, as well as its natural beauty, with wonder and enthusiasm.

TRAVELING AROUND NORTH AMERICA

Yuen Lee
Taiwan

How do you like to spend your vacation time? Do you stay at home with your family and friends? Do you study? How would you like to try something else? Why don't you take a trip to relax and get away from the stress of work or the pressures of school?

A trip around the United States would be an opportunity for you to broaden your knowledge, learn more about American culture, and communicate with people in a society different from your own. If you are interested in geography, you could experience the variety of this unique continent . . . its beautiful landscapes and interesting geological formations.

You can gain knowledge through seeing things firsthand, something which you could never accomplish in a college library or university classroom. You can also enjoy yourself because traveling in and around the United States is fun and uncomplicated; there are well-developed highways, convenient transportation systems, and easy accommodations everywhere.

The trip you decide to take depends only on such factors as your wallet, your personality, and the length of your vacation. A satisfactory journey is easy to design, with a little study and exploration before you go. You can't go wrong . . . you can only gain from the experience.

Deciding on a Destination and Planning an Itinerary

If you have no idea about where you want to go, talk to friends or visit a library. Recent issues of travel magazines will give you some ideas and travel hints. Once you have an idea about where you'd like to go, you can find a story about the place you are thinking of by looking in an index to *National Geographic Magazine* or *Travel-Holidays,* or you can look up the places that interest you most in the *Reader's Guide to Periodical Literature*. Colorful picture books about the United States in the travel sections of bookstores will also give you suggestions on destinations.

If you are currently outside the United States and would like to get information on places to see in the United States, just write the United States Travel and Tour Administration. The address of the main office is:

United States Travel and Tour Administration
Department of Commerce
14th and Constitution Avenue Northwest
Washington, D.C. 20230.

If you are currently in the United States, they will probably refer you to the National Tour Association, a private organization that can give you information on any of the travel and tour companies in North America. You can get their current phone number and address by calling 1-800-555-1212. This association, in turn, has the phone numbers and addresses of almost all tour operators in Canada and Mexico, as well as in the United States.

California alone has around thirty companies which manage tours. Just tell the National Tour Association what kind of tour you're interested in, and they will recommend companies which manage those kinds of tours. Call the numbers that they give you to get information on rates and accommodations.

Deciding on Your Means of Transportation

You can travel by private automobile or by public transportation, such as the bus or train. You can also travel by plane, if you can afford it, or by plane for long distances and a rented car for the shorter ones. Flying is fast, efficient, and generally expensive. The bus takes longer and is less comfortable, but it is less expensive and can get you to many parts of the United States that would be impossible to reach by air or train.

Bus tours can be arranged. The buses used for such tours are normally heated in winter and air-conditioned in the summer and have reclining seats with large tinted glass windows. All arrangements will be made for you, so that you won't have to worry about a thing. If you are organizing a trip for a group, twenty to forty people for example, most bus companies will be delighted to help you organize it, make reservations for hotels and sightseeing, and furnish the round-trip motorcoach transportation.

If you don't want a tour but just want the chance to see the United States at your own pace, you may want to look into purchasing a seven-day, fifteen-day, or even thirty-day bus pass with the Greyhound Bus Company or a similar bus line. Long bus trips can be boring marathons of endurance, however, and some bus terminals are located in the high-crime areas of cities and towns. Still, if you want to see a lot but don't want to drive, traveling by bus is preferable. It is inexpensive and affords you almost as much freedom as a car.

Since fares are constantly changing, check for the current, least expensive fares when you call for reservations. Because of the frequency of changing fares and the proliferation of special fares, the employees sometimes get rather confused. Always repeat the information back to the bus employee to make sure that you heard it right; then double-check a few days later with a second phone call or when you actually buy your tickets.

If you have a driver's license and access to a car, you can drive. This is still the most convenient and least expensive way to travel, especially when you are accompanied by a few friends who can also drive. Take turns, so that driving will not be a heavy load on one driver. Several friends and I took a six-day trip from Los Angeles to Vancouver. It cost us approximately $200 for gas and oil. Split five ways, that came to only $40 per person.

If you don't have a car, you can rent one. The rate depends on what kind of vehicle you need, how long you plan to keep it, and the special weekend or holiday rates available. You need to call various companies and then make your selection. Gas and oil are not expensive, especially if you choose an economy car. It is also wise to get insurance with a rental car.

If you are a car owner, consider joining the American Automobile Association (AAA). The AAA provides excellent travel services; you can get a free travel package, which includes updated maps and tourbooks. These will give you all of the information that you will need to go anywhere in the United States.

The AAA tourbooks can help you in many ways. Revised annually, they are dependable guides to Canada, Mexico, and the United States. The first half of each tourbook is primarily a sightseeing guide and gives you a general description of each state or province. Then you will find a number of indexes which refer you to points of interest, country inns, historical establishments, and resorts. The remaining half of each tourbook lists AAA-approved overnight lodging with rates and facilities, as well as AAA-approved restaurants. Tourbooks on Canadian provinces contain special information about crossing the border between the United States and Canada.

The AAA also provides small booklets on major cities called *Citibooks*. In addition to the general descriptions, they tell you what to see, where to stay, and where to dine. They also suggest interesting things for children to do, offer hints on climate and clothing, and inform you of special events.

If you like to go on picnics, the AAA also provides books on bicycling, boating, and camping areas, which also include information on permits and fees.

Fine-Tuning Your Travel Plans

Your trip will be enjoyable if you do your homework before you go. Here are some assignments!

1. Do background reading on the area in advance.

2. Make a list of attractions and sites in order of preference.

3. Mark locations on the map. Use a colored marking pen to trace your routes, trying to take as many scenic routes as time permits rather than the most direct routes.

4. Make a note of the opening and closing hours of museums and attractions.

5. Have a mechanic check your car before you leave.

Preparing What You Need for a Happy Journey

Here are some items which you may need when you travel in the United States, or in

Mexico, or Canada:

1. Identification — Is your passport up to date? Do you have an international driver's license or a valid license from the state where you live? Make sure that you ask your travel agent or the AAA what you will need should you plan to travel *outside* the United States.

2. Maps and Guidebooks — Keep maps, guidebooks, and all needed documents and information in a single, convenient location.

3. Money and Clothing — Before you pack, place your clothing on the bed and money on the table. Take only half the clothes but twice the money.

4. Food — If you have a car, carry an electric cooker or immersion heater and your own coffee, tea, dried soup, and an ice chest full of food. It is a good way to save time and money. Always taste the regional cooking, but forget the hamburgers.

5. A Swiss Army Knife — A Swiss Army knife with a corkscrew, bottle opener, scissors, tweezers, and a toothpick could become your most reliable friend on your trip.

6. Camera — A trip without a camera would be regrettable. Take along your favorite lenses, and don't forget the flash. Make sure that you have the correct ASA number marked. Don't leave your camera in the hot sun, in a car or bus, or unattended anywhere.

7. Medicine — Prepare a small medical kit which includes aspirin, a small bottle of alcohol, some cotton balls, and bandages.

8. Entertainment — Easy-to-carry games and a few good books and magazines will help you to kill the boredom of traveling a long distance.

Continuing Your Research on the Journey

When you arrive at your destination, ask the hotel desk clerk if anything special is happening in the area. There may be a festival which you did not learn about when you were doing your research at home. Always try to chat with other travelers. They may have seen something which you may want to see and be able to give you suggestions. It is also a good chance to practice your English.

Doing this will also lead to understanding American traditions and culture. On a trip to Mongolia once, I visited a Mongolian family in their tent. I drank their special tea mixed with lamb oil, ate their fried rice, and listened to the traditionally dressed Mongolians talking about their lives. I was completely fascinated to be part of a world so different from my own. It was an unforgettable journey and different from any trip which I have made in the United States. In Mongolia there were no cups of coffee or skyscrapers, and here there are no tents to sip tea and eat fried rice in, unless you happen to go camping. Yet the principles of good traveling remain the same. Plan, but be flexible!

As Francis Bacon once said, "Travel in the younger sort, is a part of education; in the elder, a part of experience." Regardless of age, you will gain both an education *and* experience. From the time you determine your destination, do your research, and plan your routes, until the moment you get back home, you will be augmenting your knowledge, experience, and happy memories.

ENJOYING THE REST OF AMERICA: A CASE STUDY

Dong K. Shin
Korea

One warm sunny October afternoon several years ago, I was sitting in my backyard in California . . . daydreaming . . . and gazing at the brightly colored autumn leaves rustling softly against the profound blue of a clear and cloudless sky.

Suddenly a leaf disengaged from a branch and floated to the ground . . . and then another . . . and another. They dissolved into a dreamy picture of my homeland, Korea, with its four distinct seasons. I could clearly picture the sparkling white snows of winter . . . the soft pink blossoms of spring . . . the rich green leaves of summer . . . and the gloriously colorful mountains and fields of autumn.

As I envisioned the landscapes of my youth, I could picture a young boy exploring vast mountains that were decorated with spectacular and abundant bursts of autumn reds, oranges, and golds. A stream gently caressed the stones and rocks as it flowed toward the ocean and filled my ears with its music. Birds sweetly sang their praises to the glory of the moment, and soft breezes rustled the leaves of the trees and propelled them like tiny parachutes of red and yellow through the air to the ground.

With the leaves of Korea, I drifted silently and softly back to my yard in California. I was overcome with longing for the familiar sounds and sights of home, a homesickness for which there was no easy cure. The reality of my situation was clear. Returning to my native country was an impossible dream.

In that moment of sadness, an alternative solution occurred to me. Perhaps I could seek comparable surroundings in my new country that would satisfy my longings for nature. I began to think of an outdoor adventure somewhere in California.

When I told my wife of my idea, she was enthusiastic. We both agreed that the best place to seek the information we needed was the American Automobile Association (AAA), where we were members.

We went to the nearest AAA the next day and asked when and where we could find gorgeous autumn scenery. Their immediate response was *Yosemite National Park*, about a day's easy drive from our home. They also told us that October through the middle of November was the best time to go and provided us with maps, brochures, and suggestions.

My wife and I decided to go, requested several days of vacation from our respective employers, and were thrilled when we both were given the same days off. We decided to camp rather than stay in a hotel. It would be less costly and bring us closer to nature. Since it was off-season, we didn't even have to make reservations for a campsite. We bought the equipment that we needed, and a week later, we were driving north on the magnificent US Highway 395 to Yosemite.

Yosemite National Park was everything that I had dreamed of and more. The park was a scenic wonderland of sculptured peaks and domes, having hundred-foot waterfalls tumbling down granite cliffs, groves of giant sequoias and forests of pine, fir, and oak, wildflowers in alpine meadows, varied species of birds and mammals, and scenic drives and trails to areas of mountain grandeur. Moreover, spectacular autumn leaves added to the beauty.

That's the story of how I started to camp in California. Since then I have enjoyed camping in many places around this state and around the whole United States. Now I'd like to share some of my camping ideas with you.

Camping is an American tradition. It started with the first settlers and continued with the pioneers. However, the concept of leisure camping is only slightly over a hundred years old. Camping is now one of the most popular recreations in America and attracts millions of Americans and non-Americans who wish to get away from all the hustle and bustle of city life and enjoy friends, family, and the proximity of nature.

American poets, artists, and philosophers have written beautifully throughout America's history about the value of nature and the outdoor experience. The American philosopher and writer Henry David Thoreau wrote these words in his famous book *Walden,* published in 1854:

> *"We need the tonic of wildness . . .*
> *to explore*
> *and learn all things . . .*
> *We can never have enough of nature.*
> *We must be refreshed by the sight of inexhaustible vigor,*
> *vast and titanic features . . .*
> *the thunder-cloud,*
> *and the rain which lasts three weeks . . .*
> *We need to witness our own limits transgressed,*
> *and some life pasturing freely . . ."*

Walt Whitman, the great American poet of the last century, was even more emphatic when he wrote in his *Leaves of Grass:*

> *"Now I see the secret of the making of the best persons. It is to*
> *grow in the open air, and to eat and sleep with the earth."*

If you weren't already convinced about the value of camping, are you now? If you are, it would be wise to find out about the experiences of others until you accumulate your own experience. Nowadays, many American communities have camping, fishing, hiking, backpacking, and cross-country ski clubs. Attending meetings of such clubs will give you an opportunity to talk with experienced campers or backpackers. The Sierra

Club is a valuable but inexpensive organization to join. It not only sponsors a variety of outings and activities, but is an excellent source of information on what camping equipment you should buy. The equipment might include a tent, sleeping bag, air mattress, a flashlight, a portable stove, a first aid kit, and maps.

Once you have the proper equipment and the right amount of know-how, you are ready to go camping. But where? California offers an unparalleled variety of landscapes, everything from sandy beaches to high mountain peaks, volcanic areas to vast desert expanses, trout streams to fresh water lakes, and beaches to thick forests. In fact, there are over 200 state parks, 5,000 lakes, and various national parks and forests in California.

AAA will be able to tell you what the required fees are, what facilities are offered, and the answers to most other questions which you may have. They can also tell you about how and where to purchase the "Golden Eagle Passport," which costs very little and will allow you an unlimited number of visits to all the national parks for an entire year.

AAA can also tell you about the current fees charged for sport fishing. According to California State Law, anyone 16 years or older who wishes to take any kind of fish, mollusk, invertebrate, amphibian, or crustacean in California must have a fishing license.

Some state and national parks, such as Yosemite National Park, will accept reservations. For parks as popular as Yosemite, making reservations is strongly recommended, especially during the summer and long weekends. You may make a reservation as early as eight weeks before the date that you expect to arrive. When you make a reservation, be prepared to state the number of persons, the ages of any children, the type of site desired, the date and estimated time of arrival, and length of stay.

While you are camping, always keep camping safety in mind. Be as careful at the campsite as you are at home, and leave the site cleaner than it was when you first arrived. Remember, too, that parks are also sanctuaries for wild animals. Respect the animals and don't feed them. The only other piece of advice is to get out and enjoy a camping experience as soon as you can.

As John Muir, the famous explorer of the Sierra Nevada and Yosemite National Park, said:

> "Climb the mountains and get their good tidings. Nature's peace will flow into you as sunshine flows into trees. The winds will blow their own freshness into you, and the storms their energy, while cares will drop off like autumn leaves."